Demons
&
Deliverance

H. A. Maxwell Whyte

Demons and Deliverance

(Formerly: *A Manual on Exorcism* and *Dominion Over Demons*)

Copyright © 1989 by Mrs. Olive Whyte
Printed in the United States of America
ISBN: 0-88368-216-8

Editorial assistance for Whitaker House by Debra Petrosky.

Cover photo and design by Terry Dugan.

Scripture quotations, unless otherwise noted, are taken from the *New King James Version,* copyright © 1979, 1980, 1982, Thomas Nelson Publishers, and used by permission.

Scripture quotations marked *KJV* are taken from the *King James Version* of the Bible.

Foreword

This book is for people who want answers. If you are seeking deliverance for yourself, this book will offer hope in the midst of darkness; if you want to learn more about deliverance but have been apprehensive about the realm of spiritual warfare, the truths here will be invaluable.

You are about to benefit from Maxwell Whyte' forty years of ministry experience. As you read and study this book, you will be given practical and scriptural tools for dealing with demonic forces. You will also learn how to open prison doors for others and help those bound and defeated by oppression, addiction, sickness, mental problems, and unexplainable behavior.

In the spiritual realm, Maxwell Whyte was a pioneer. Sovereignly led by the Holy Spirit in 1948 into an understanding of demonic activity and spiritual warfare, Maxwell embarked on a journey in ministry that was fraught with uncertainty and an absence of familiar landmarks. As is so often the case with pioneers, Maxwell was misunderstood, ridiculed, and ostracized by the Christian community, even in his own city! Despite great opposition, Maxwell forged ahead in the battle against the forces of Satan, convinced that the ministry of deliverance was scripturally based and was being restored to the church in his day.

In 1950 Maxwell began to record his experiences, and over the next two and a half decades he authored eighteen books. His first book, *The Power of the Blood,* was widely distributed throughout the world, selling over 300,000 copies, and has been translated into several languages. In fact, this life-changing message has just been translated into Chinese and will be distributed throughout the Chinese speaking world. Although Maxwell was aware of the project, he did not live to see its fulfillment as the Lord called him home in May of 1988.

The edition you now hold in your hands is a compilation of two earlier books by Maxwell Whyte, *Dominion Over Demons* and *A Manual on Exorcism*. Prompted by continual requests for these two books, the publisher realized the need to once again make them available to the Christian community. The message of freedom they proclaim is needed now more than ever in this age of increased demonic activity, and I am honored as Maxwell's son to pen the foreword to this revised edition.

Today I have the privilege of pastoring the church that Maxwell Whyte pastored for thirty-one years. I grew up in that church, and I now have the responsibility to entrust to others the same truths that Dad taught me. He has blazed a trail ahead of us to make it much more acceptable to proclaim and practice the ministry of deliverance. Maxwell has made an invaluable contribution to the Body of Christ around the world in the understanding and reality of spiritual warfare. He was not only my natural father, he was also my spiritual father, and to him I owe a debt of gratitude.

Jesus said, "The works that I do, [you] will do also; and greater works than these will [you] do, because I go to My Father" (John 14:12). The time has come for the church to take up the mantle of ministry that Jesus carried and declare to the world that there is sight for the blind, restoration for the broken-hearted, and deliverance for the captives. May the truths of this book help to precipitate such an awakening.

Stephen Whyte
Senior Pastor
Dayspring Christian Fellowship
Scarborough, Ontario, Canada

Contents

Part One: Dominion Over Demons

Part Two: Questions and Answers

> 1. What is a demon?
> 2. How does a person come under the influence
>   of demons in the first place?
> 3. How can you know when you have a demon?
> 4. What is deliverance?
> 5. Can just anybody cast out demons?

> 1. Can a Christian be possessed by a demon?
> 2. If not possessed, is there any other sense in
>   which a Christian might "have" a demon?
> 3. Where does the Bible say that a Christian can
>   have a demon?

4. How could a demon and the Holy Spirit dwell in the same person at the same time?

5. How can we be sure that any Christian's manifestation of the Holy Spirit is genuine, if Christians can have demons?

6. Was the apostle Paul's thorn in the flesh a demon?

7. How can a Christian resist the demonic influences that surround him?

8. How can you keep from giving a "place" to the devil?

1. Are there demons that cause sickness?

2. When a person is sick, should you always cast out a demon?

3. If a person has been set free from a demon that has caused sickness, should he immediately give up all medication?

4. Are there demons that cause emotional disturbances, or are such problems merely psychological?

5. Are there certain kinds of demons that may contaminate us through experimentation with the occult?

6. Are there demons that can come to us through our ancestors?

7. Could there be such a thing as a "dormant demon" that might not manifest itself until a certain time in a person's life?

8. Are some demons stronger than others?

9. Is it safe to listen to what demons say?

3. Isn't it mentally unhealthy to become too "demon conscious"?
4. Can't demons be handled more effectively by simply praising God and ignoring them?
5. Doesn't the ministry of deliverance magnify the devil rather than Jesus Christ?
6. Why blame the works of the flesh on demons?
7. If the ministry of deliverance is valid and scriptural, where has it been throughout the church age?
8. Wouldn't it be better to cast the demons out of ourselves, rather than worrying about the demons in others?
9. If the great archangel Michael dared not rebuke Satan, who are we that we may do so?

Preface

My first experience with the ministry of deliverance involved a man who had suffered from chronic asthma from birth. Before he came to us for prayer, he had been prayed for by the orthodox methods known to the church at that time, but nothing at all happened. When we changed from the prayer of petition to a prayer of forceful command, the results were astounding.

As soon as we *commanded* the asthma to leave in Jesus' name, the spirit of infirmity causing the asthmatic symptoms began to come out. In an hour and a half, he was completely and permanently healed.

To say that my wife and I were astonished is an understatement. We had not done this by knowledge of theology, for what does theology teach us about casting out demons? We did it experimentally, willing to try any method or system that would bring release to the afflicted.

This first clear-cut case of healing by deliverance brought us a glimmer of understanding on a subject about which we knew practically nothing. This formed a basis of experimentation, and during the next three decades we were to have some intensely interesting cases and many marvelous deliverances. God taught us progressively by His Holy Spirit as we were willing to tackle each case presented to us.

I took the simple position of knowing nothing—but I was willing to learn by successes and mistakes. We made many errors, but we saw some wonderful deliverances. Fortunately, I had not been taught that a Christian cannot "have" a demon. In fact, I had been taught *nothing* for or against demons; I was just plain ignorant.

More and more suffering people approached us over the years as news leaked out that we were involved in the "deliverance ministry." Most of them seemed to be completely, or at least partially, delivered. Some were untouched, even though we were willing to spend much time in trying to dislodge the demons that were troubling them. We rejoiced at the successes but continued to ask the Lord about the failures. The Lord gradually taught us, and our percentage of successes increased.

We learned many things, but there is so much more to know. The whole ministry of deliverance seems to be an inexhaustible well of God's love to set the captives free.

I would urge the reader to consider the author not as an expert, but merely as a servant of God whom the Lord has brought into a knowledge of this vital subject. Because of this ministry, thousands have been set free and are still being set free.

This is not a theoretical theology, but a practical, down-to-earth Bible approach to the needs of people—and it works!

H.A. Maxwell Whyte

Part One

Dominion Over Demons

1
Satanic Realities

While I was preaching in the auditorium of the City Hall in Hamilton, Bermuda, a Scottish lady in the crowd listened intently to the message of healing and deliverance. Several months later she visited our church in Toronto and asked for prayer for her arthritis. I had been informed, however, that this lady regularly attended a spiritist church and had no connection whatsoever with the Christian faith. Her desperate need for healing, however, made her a sincere inquirer.

I explained that I must be frank and asked her if it was true that she was attending spiritist services and seances.

"Yes," she said, "and I have received so much benefit from the meetings. I have found God in a much closer way, and He has helped me so much."

I gently explained to her that all forms of the occult are expressly forbidden in the Scriptures. God said that all who participate in these activities will actually be cut off or severed from His presence—which was quite the opposite of her testimony about how close she felt to God.

"Would you like me to show you in the Bible where all forms of spiritism are expressly forbidden by God?" I asked.

"Yes, please show me." Her openness indicated that the Holy Spirit was at work. I turned to the following Bible passages:

> "Give no regard to mediums and familiar spirits; do not seek after them, to be defiled by them: I am the Lord"—Leviticus 19:31.

> "And the person who turns after mediums and familiar spirits, to prostitute himself with them, I will set My face against that person and cut him off from his people"—Leviticus 20:6.

> And when they say to you, "Seek those who are mediums and wizards, who whisper and mutter," should not a people seek their God? Should they seek the dead on behalf of the living? To the law and to the testimony! If they do not speak according to this word, it is because there is no light in them—Isaiah 8:19,20.

Those passages quickly convinced her. She immediately renounced all forms of occultism and necromancy. This woman had *no idea* that God had forbidden these practices, and she was very humble about the whole matter.

When I prayed for her, the Lord instantly healed her of all arthritis, stiffness, and pain, and she kept her healing. A week after her deliverance, she returned to the church and was mightily baptized in the Holy Spirit, speaking in tongues. She wrote to me regularly from Scotland, and her faith remained firm.

Weird Demonic Powers

Those who practice spiritism and the occult have produced amazing, verifiable signs and wonders. To deny their power is foolishness. Things can be made to appear and disappear.

Levitation of inanimate objects is a reality. Articles such as vases and drinking glasses can sail across a room and be dashed in pieces against a wall. Tables can be made to walk up walls, and voices, including "other tongues," can be heard through trumpets and other objects.

I remember speaking to a Jewish friend who had been in the company of several men in Newcastle, Australia, one of whom practiced the occult arts. He boasted that he could cause anything to appear in the room where they were sitting.

My friend immediately asked him to "materialize" a tuna fish out of the Southern Ocean. No sooner had the wish been made known, than a great, flapping, wet tuna was right in the middle of the room.

How did it get there? How can a fish appear out of nowhere? How are inanimate objects levitated, defying the natural laws of gravity? Are all these lying signs and wonders so much "hocus pocus," or are they real?

The answer, my friends, is that *they are real, but they are not of God.* They are brought about through demon powers. The demons, being invisible, carry the glasses, support the walking tables upon the walls, and transport such things as a tuna fish out of the sea into a room. They have laws that we do not know and understand. Anyone who opens their lives, through disobedience to God's Holy Word, can become the servants of these same demon powers.

The two magicians in Pharaoh's court, Jannes and Jambres, like modern African witch doctors, had limited power—but power nonetheless. Moses' rod turned into a serpent, and theirs appeared to do likewise. (See Exodus 7:10-12.)

But we must remember that Satan has no power to create. Only God can and does create by His Word. Satan can create nothing except confusion and havoc by taking the things of God and prostituting them to his own ends.

We do not believe that Jannes and Jambres created serpents; we believe they merely used demon powers to transport them from the forests into Pharaoh's court. The serpent created by God then ate up the natural-born serpents, showing that God is greater than the devil and his demon powers.

Good and Bad Spirits?

Man communicates with demons, and he thinks it's merely a parlor game or harmless fun. Many people believe in "white magic" and "black magic" and distinguish between "good spirits" and "bad spirits." The truth is that many bad spirits pretend to be good in order to deceive. All demons are bad, even if they transform themselves into angels of light. (See 2 Corinthians 11:14.)

People have many misconceptions regarding spiritist mediums and what actually happens at seances. Regardless of what they claim, spiritist mediums do not communicate with the dead. Instead, they communicate with demon spirits who imitate those who have died.

Imagine a person being inhabited by a demon for years. On his death, this demon roams around in a disembodied state looking for another person who will not resist his efforts to gain entrance. This demon knows many intimate things that happened in the life of the departed person. If some medium is willing to communicate with this familiar spirit, naturally the spirit can simulate the dead person and fool the assembled gullible gathering.

Many people also have misconceptions about haunted houses. Some think that the ghosts of departed people live in such houses, but this is not true.

Demons haunt houses and can cause thumps and bangs at any time of the night or day. These happenings are real, but a Christian need not fear them because he has the name of Jesus and His shed blood with which to expel these demon powers.

Increased Satanic Activity

I read recently that every American high school has its witch or witches. In the Bible, men who dabble in the occult are called wizards. Both male and female witches are possessed by a "familiar spirit," which is expressly forbidden by Scripture.

> There shall not be found among you anyone . . . who practices witchcraft, or a soothsayer, or one who interprets omens, or a sorcerer, or one who conjures spells, or a medium, or a spiritist, or one who calls up the dead. For all who do these things are an abomination to the Lord—Deuteronomy 18:10-12.

Spiritism is now openly practiced on every American campus. Witchcraft is widespread in Britain, and Brazil faces an epidemic of occultism. Why is there such an increase in satanic activity? Because people are departing from God and His Word, and the vacuum created in the human spirit is being filled by "other spirits."

A beautiful sixteen-year-old girl once approached me for prayer. She seemed the type you would meet at church, but Satan is an arch deceiver. This girl first told me that she had been on drugs. Then she confessed that she had also been acting as a witch at school. Apparently she had two demons.

I laid my hands upon her head, rebuked the demons, and commanded them to come out in Jesus' name. Immediately they started to scream, for they realized their impotency before the name of Jesus and His shed blood. They screamed and choked her for nearly an hour. Many surprised Christian students began to intercede for her until she was completely delivered.

I asked her if she would like to be filled with the Holy Spirit. She readily agreed, and she was taught to plead and honor the blood of Jesus in prayer. Soon the Holy Spirit entered into her, and she began to speak in a beautiful unknown tongue! I marveled at the wonderful change that Jesus brought to her countenance.

In Need of Deliverance

I realize that some of these accounts may shock those "who are at ease in Zion" (Amos 6:1). While the bridegroom delayed, the church slumbered, slept, and lost many of these great truths. (See Matthew 25:5.) Today, however, God is bringing deliverance. Precious secrets that were unknown for years are being revealed by the Spirit of God.

How many Christians are indeed wrestling against demon powers? How many are arrayed in their gospel armor? Our churches look more like social clubs than military barracks! We neither know our enemy, nor the weapons that God gives us to fight him. We don't want to fight the forces that oppose the kingdom of God; we prefer to dream about going to heaven.

Many people attending our churches today are themselves in need of deliverance. Many are bound and oppressed, and some of their peculiar mannerisms *may* be due to demonic influence.

One Sunday morning, I was ministering in a full gospel church in Brooklyn, New York. The pastor and his wife had recently graduated from a Bible school in Lima, New York. He was leading a song service, when suddenly a woman in the congregation began to sway from side to side with a look of contortion and agony spread across her face. She started to bump into those on either side of her, and it was obvious to me that she was in torment.

Turning to the pastor, I commented, "See that woman down there? That's a first-class case of a religious demon operating."

"What should we do?" the startled young pastor asked.

In a situation like that, the gifts of the Spirit are indispensable. The Lord impressed upon me to walk down the aisle and speak to the woman. At that point, however, I did not know what God wanted me to say to her. I encouraged the pastor to continue the singing while I addressed the situation.

"Sister, you are tormented," I said to her.

"Yes," she replied, "I know."

Then I offered to pray for her during the time of ministry that followed the service. Before returning to the front, I told her to sit down and behave in the name of the Lord, which she did.

At the end of the service my wife and I approached the lady and asked her if she wanted us to pray for her. She did, so I began to rebuke the religious demon in Jesus' name. Immediately, it started to scream with an unearthly sound. I quickly circled the sanctuary and closed every window. It was summertime, and the church members—not to mention their next door neighbors—were astonished at what was happening.

By the time I returned from this chore, my wife laid her hands on the woman's shoulders and held her from being hurled to the floor. The demons in this woman were greatly agitated. After about ten minutes of screaming and violent coughing, she was delivered.

After experiencing a glorious release from demonic bondage, she immediately asked, "Why hasn't anyone ever done this for me before?" What a pathetic question—and yet how appropriate. Why?

The ministry of deliverance, or casting out demons, has been neglected by the Christian church for a number of reasons. Many ministers and churches shy away from it because they fear the unknown. God is restoring scriptural teaching on deliverance to equip people for this ministry in the latter days.

Where Do Demons Come From?

Many people lack knowledge of the nature and operation of demons. Most Christians know that angels are ministering spirits sent to those who are the heirs of salvation. (See Hebrews 1:14; Psalms 91:11.) Unfortunately, we often forget about the opposing spiritual forces in the world. Evil angels—those who fell from their previous high estate as the trusted servants of Jehovah—were defeated in their rebellion and cast out of heaven with Lucifer, the son of the morning, or Satan himself.

> So the great dragon was cast out, that serpent of old, called the Devil and Satan, who deceives the whole world; he was cast to the earth, and *his angels were cast out with him*—Revelation 12:9, italics added.

The Bible also teaches that the Lord used these fallen angels to visit suffering upon those who deliberately disobeyed Him.

> He [God] cast on them the fierceness of His anger, wrath, indignation, and trouble, by sending *angels of destruction* among them—Psalm 78:49.

The next verse implies that these evil angels caused a deadly plague that brought God's judgment. These fallen angels are "reserved in everlasting chains under darkness for the judgment of the great day" (Jude 6). At the coming of the Lord Jesus Christ, Satan himself will be bound for one thousand years and cast into the bottomless pit. (See Revelation 20:1-3.)

When Satan was cast out of heaven with his legions, he was given authority over mankind and all creation. In fact, he is able to influence everything that has life. And he has a very definite effect on the very atmosphere that surrounds the earth. The apostle Paul called him the "prince of the power of the air" (Ephesians 2:2).

This beautiful, created being was at one time called Lucifer, which means "Shining One." (See Isaiah 14:12.) He held the greatest position among the created angelic hosts but tried to usurp God's throne. Lucifer proudly made a five-fold declaration:

> I will ascend into heaven, I will exalt my throne above the stars of God; I will also sit on the mount of the congregation on the farthest sides of the north; I will ascend above the heights of the clouds, I will be like the Most High—Isaiah 14:13,14.

Lucifer did not lose his power or authority when he was cast out of heaven. By divine permission he uses it today among the earthly creation. His power, therefore, is second only to Jesus Christ and is infinitely greater than many people imagine.

In the end, however, Satan will meet a resounding defeat. That same passage of Scripture goes on to describe the judgment of Lucifer.

> Yet you [Lucifer] shall be brought down to Sheol, to the lowest depths of the Pit. Those who see you will gaze at you, and consider you, saying: "Is this the man who made the earth tremble, who shook kingdoms, who made the world as a wilderness and destroyed its cities, who did not open the house of his prisoners?"—Isaiah 14:15-17.

Wicked Spirits

Christians must remember that Satan is neither omnipresent nor omniscient. His power is limited. In order to carry on his insidious work of maintaining curses upon the world, he uses a great company of wicked spirits, or fallen angels, to do his bidding. Without a doubt these wicked spirits are governed by well disciplined angelic orders of generals and captains.

We do not know the number of these wicked spirits. There seems little doubt that they are far more numerous than mankind. The poor demoniac of Gadara had a legion in him. We read in *Smith's Standard Bible Dictionary* that a legion consists of about 6,000 men and expresses any large number, with the accessory ideas of order and subordination. (See Matthew 26:53; Mark 5:9.)

There seems little doubt that many accidents, misfortunes, quarrels, sicknesses, diseases, and unhappiness are the *direct* result of the individual work of one or more wicked spirits.

Spirits are just as much *beings* as humans, except that they have no physical form. This is why they seek to indwell humans or animals (as in the case of the swine into which the Lord cast the legion from the demoniac of Gadara). They may even seek to re-enter a body when the spirit of that person ceases to resist their forces. (See Matthew 12:43-45.)

Who Fills the Empty Spaces?

Dr. Lawrence Hammond, a born-again nuclear scientist, tells of an experience that changed his thinking about demonic power.

> One sun-drenched day in voodoo-infested Haiti, an old hag violently attacked me. Her face was a horrible Halloween mask, her teeth fangs, her fingers clutching claws. Nobody had to tell me that she was oppressed by demons. Through the power of the blood of Jesus, and the authority of His name, the Holy Spirit enabled me to cast the demons out of her.

I had never heard of anyone practicing deliverance today. Furthermore, I knew that many Christians totally rejected the existence of demons. But face to face with the satanic power expressed through this violent woman, I learned—much to my amazement—that a Christian who believes he has received power over the enemy can cast out evil spirits in the name of Jesus.

But I had a lot to learn. For weeks I puzzled over how that woman could be so oppressed by demons.

As a scientist, I knew the emptiness of the atom, whose electrons are so small that only one millionth part of that atomic volume is occupied. I also knew that the human body is composed of such "empty" atoms, and that you and I are actually 999,999,999,999 parts empty space!

Lee Chesnut, former nuclear science lecturer and author of *The Atom Speaks and Echoes the Word of God,* pointed out that this emptiness must be filled with something: either the Spirit of God or the spirit of Satan. As he said, "You and I must decide between Satan and the Lord Jesus Christ, and which is to occupy and fill our lives."

Oppressed, Obsessed, or Afflicted

When evil spirits gain entrance into a person's body, we speak of *demon oppression.* These demons use the body of the afflicted person to work their wicked acts. Demons delight in actually controlling humans and speaking through them.

Demons can worry, tempt, or distract believers. This would be another example of *demon oppression.* They might cause us to get "out of victory," or lose our temper, a condition in which no Christian need ever be.

If evil spirits control a person's mind, this is called *demon obsession*. Someone who thinks he has committed the unpardonable sin is plagued by demon obsession. Upon questioning, however, he is unable to tell you what constitutes the unpardonable sin!

Demons also cause many afflictions from which mankind suffers. The spirits described in the Scriptures are foul, wicked, evil, deaf, dumb, infirm, unclean, and seducing.

Many believe that cancer is nothing more than a work of evil spirits which, when cast out in the mighty name of Jesus, shrivel up and die. Who disputes the possibility that arthritis, tumors, deafness, and dumbness may not be the actual work of demons in portions of the body? We do not say that such a person is "demon possessed," but we do suggest that they are sorely afflicted by demons.

We believe that the primary cause of all sickness is spiritual. Symptoms may be treated by natural means, yet if we use the name of Jesus Christ and His shed blood as a weapon against Satan in faith, then certainly we will see manifestations of divine healing because the sickness is destroyed at the root.

Deal with Demons First

Are healing and deliverance the same? Jesus didn't think so. He distinctly differentiated between divine healing and deliverance from demons. Let's look at His last discourse to His disciples. He taught them to expect *five* signs to prove the ministry of the Word of God.

> And these signs will follow those who believe: In My name they will cast out demons; they will speak with new tongues; they will take up serpents; and if they drink anything deadly, it will by no means hurt them; they will lay hands on the sick, and they will recover—Mark 16:17,18.

The first sign was casting out demons in His name. This particular sign is mentioned *before* the sign of physical healing. We do not know whether this order is accidental, but we suspect that Jesus had a reason for listing deliverance first because He always dealt with primary issues first. If we first cast out demons, we would frequently have no need to pray for the sick; deliverance from the demon would bring all the healing needed.

It is interesting to note that the very first recorded act of public ministry by Jesus was to cast out a devil.

> Now there was a man in their synagogue with an unclean spirit. And he cried out, saying, "Let us alone! What have we to do with You, Jesus of Nazareth? Did You come to destroy us? I know who You are—the Holy One of God!"
>
> But Jesus rebuked him, saying, "Be quiet, and come out of him!" And when the unclean spirit had convulsed him and cried out with a loud voice, he came out of him.
>
> Then they were all amazed, so that they questioned among themselves, saying, "What is this? What new doctrine is this? For with authority He commands even the unclean spirits, and they obey Him"—Mark 1:23-26.

Many in the church today are asking these same questions. What is deliverance? Is this some new doctrine? Is every believer called to deliver people from evil spirits? Are there dangers in getting involved in deliverance?

This ministry raises many questions in the minds of Christians. Can a born-again Christian be oppressed by demon powers? Are physical and mental sicknesses caused by demons? Where has this ministry of deliverance been throughout the ages? Can a Christian cast demons out of himself? How does a person come under demon influence?

The time has come to answer the questions Christians are asking today. Not so we can formulate more doctrine and theology, but so we can start setting people free!

If this ministry was so important to Jesus, should it be any less important to us?

2

The Strange World of Spirits

"You foul spirit of fear, come out of her in Jesus' Name!" I commanded. I knew that nothing else would help her.

At the close of a home prayer meeting in Florida, a few people had decided to stay for the prayer of deliverance. A fearful woman who had been troubled with a stiff neck for many years was among those in need of ministry. I began to pray by commanding the spirit of fear to come out of her. Immediately we witnessed a reaction, and for the next few minutes this spirit began to choke out of her until peace returned.

Then God reminded her how she had been afflicted with this miserable condition in the first place. When she was five years old, her father frequently told her scary bedtime stories. One night he outdid himself in horror fiction. The details were so vivid and frightening that she began to scream in terror. The mother rushed in and commanded her well-meaning husband to leave the room. She tried to comfort her terrified daughter, but it was too late; the damage had been done. When her mother left the room, the little girl buried herself beneath a patchwork quilt, completely petrified with fear at the memory of her father's gruesome story.

As a result of this terrifying experience, a spirit of fear entered this young girl. This foul spirit remained for fifty years and also brought a spirit of tension, causing stiffness in the neck. She experienced great relief when we cast that demon out of her.

Man—A Spiritual Being

The ministry of deliverance is difficult for some people to understand. Let's turn to the Scriptures to explain the spiritual realm.

The apostle Paul prayed, "May the God of peace Himself sanctify you completely; and may your whole spirit, soul, and body be preserved blameless at the coming of our Lord Jesus Christ" (1 Thessalonians 5:23). Man is triune. First spirit, then soul, then body. Man is, therefore, primarily and essentially a spiritual being.

In the beginning, God fashioned a human body out of the dust of this earth, and then breathed into this lifeless body the breath of life. I do not believe that God merely expanded Adam's lungs with fresh air. Obviously, it would take more than this to cause him to live. I believe that God literally breathed into man His own life. He breathed *spirit* into him, for God *is* Spirit.

Man is first a spiritual being. God did not create man to use his mind apart from his spirit. Unfortunately, our modern educational systems appeal only to the development of the mind. The mind of man teaches the mind of man, but the spirit of man is completely ignored. In fact, unregenerate men simply do not comprehend their spiritual needs at all. As the Scriptures say,

> The natural man does not receive the things of the Spirit of God, for they are foolishness to him; nor can he know them, because they are spiritually discerned—1 Corinthians 2:14.

The mind can understand only the things of the mind, and likewise the spirit the things of the Spirit. An old adage states that "Birds of a feather flock together." Like always goes with like.

A church that ministers to the needs of the human spirit will attract spiritual people. But most religion simply caters to the carnal man. The body, with its five senses, prefers to produce a substitute for true worship. But Jesus said that God is looking for those who will worship Him "in *spirit* and truth" (John 4:23, italics added).

We cannot worship God with our minds or intellects—with the efforts of soulish religion. Long ago Job asked, "Can you search out the deep things of God?" (Job 11:7) The answer is *No*. We cannot find God or understand anything about God with our minds or our bodies. That's why God made man a spiritual being.

The Door to the Spiritual Realm

Like goes to like. "Deep calls unto deep" (Psalm 42:7). If man wishes to find God, he must seek Him through his spirit. If we want to listen to a radio program, we must tune the frequency of our receiver to exactly the same frequency as that of the transmitter. In this way, we can get perfect reception if we are in range. In like manner, the spiritual part of our triune nature can communicate with God when we are tuned in through the working of the Holy Spirit.

When we commune with God, we do so with our spirits. Only then do we begin to understand the mind of God. We begin to realize that God gives us some of His mind. (See 1 Corinthians 2:16.) We begin to think as God thinks, but only in part, of course. Our minds become actuated by our regenerated spirit in communion with God.

This actuating of our minds becomes quickened when we are baptized in the Holy Spirit. We begin to understand how God imparts such gifts as words of wisdom or knowledge, discerning of spirits, tongues, interpretation, and prophecy. These come from the Spirit of God through the human spirit—not through the mind.

If spiritual gifts came through our minds, then it could be said that "we just thought them up." But since they come down from God, we do not think them up at all; we simply receive them through our spirits. Any so-called gift that comes only from the human mind is a counterfeit gift.

On either side of the spirit of man are two spiritual powers vying for his attention. On the one hand God and the angels exert a holy influence on man. On the other hand Satan, who left his state of perfection to become the devil, tempts men to sin. Many believe that he took with him one-third of all the created angelic beings, and that these now constitute the demons that torment and afflict all mankind. Lucifer and God's angels became Satan and his demons.

Once a man experiences the new birth and learns the secret of using his spirit instead of his mind, he opens the door into the spiritual realm. He may now communicate with other spiritual beings—and this is spiritual dynamite! By the operation of his own free will, he may freely converse with Almighty God. Some Christians have even experienced visitations from the angels.

Satanic Voices

Man, being essentially a spiritual being, can hear the voice of God's Spirit or the voice of Satan and his evil hordes. Many clear-minded, Holy Spirit baptized Christians have been disturbed at the suggestions that evil spirits place in their minds. In fact, those who excessively dwell on such thoughts have even suffered nervous breakdowns. Other believers who are not firmly grounded in the Word of God have doubted their salvation and ultimately lost their minds because of this mental torment.

The moment we open the door of our spirit to the spiritual realm, we can receive whatever voice we tune into. For example, a short-wave radio receiver does not differentiate between Russian stations or American stations; it simply hears what it tunes into. The human spirit acts in the same way. But with a radio, we can tune out radio Moscow if we do not like the propaganda. Similarly, Christians can tune out the unwanted satanic voices and tune into God's frequency by an act of their will.

Many Christian people have told us about the evil, unrighteous, and lustful ideas that Satan injects into their thought life. Other believers report that Satan says they are not saved. But the Word of God says just the opposite. Which are we to believe? The Spirit of God bears witness to the Scriptures that say we are saved by faith. On the other hand, Satan protests, "Oh no, you're not!" Isn't this the same strategy the devil used in the garden of Eden? "Hath God said . . . ?" What a liar he is!

Remember, hearing a satanic voice is not wrong. Sin comes only in obeying that voice. Never become obsessed with the voice of the enemy. People who continue to listen to Satan are rapidly on their way to becoming demon obsessed. Believers must deal quickly and decisively with the lies of the enemy. Arm yourself with the Word of God and refuse to believe anything contrary to its teaching.

Deceived by Satan

Unless a believer maintains his integrity and his righteous standing before God, he can easily be seduced by an angel of light. (See 1 Timothy 4:1; 2 Corinthians 11:13-15.) These evil spirits attempt to woo Christians in much the same way as an immoral woman would endeavor to win the affections of a married man.

The difficulty is that Satan doesn't always tell lies. An angel of light may actually tell the truth, but its unholy inspiration comes directly from Satan. Many Christians who attend church regularly are being deceived by these angels of light and are sources of grave trouble to their pastors.

The New Testament records one such incident that Paul and Silas encountered in Philippi.

> Now it happened, as we went to prayer, that a certain slave girl possessed with a spirit of divination met us, who brought her masters much profit by fortune-telling.
> This girl followed Paul and us, and cried out, saying, "These men are the servants of the Most High God, who proclaim to us the way of salvation." And this she did for many days—Acts 16:16,17.

Notice that the slave girl's declaration was correct—Paul and Silas were God's messengers who preached salvation. Many unwary people in full gospel churches today would have applauded such an utterance as being of the Holy Spirit. After all, it was *true,* wasn't it? But Paul, being greatly annoyed, turned and said *to the spirit,* "I command you in the name of Jesus Christ to come out of her." And he came out that very hour. (See Acts 16:18.)

No wonder Jesus told His disciples to be "wise as serpents and harmless as doves" (Matthew 10:16). We continually need to be one step ahead of Satan so that his seducing spirits do not deceive us.

Testing the Spirits

Many questionable teachings are floating around in the church during these last days.

Beware of doctrines that throw doubt on the reality of heaven and hell and God's judgments; doctrines that tell us no one lives again until the resurrection day. These doctrines are not revealed by the Holy Spirit, whom Jesus said would guide us into all truth. Such doctrines are revealed by other spirits.

Now the Spirit expressly says that in latter times some will depart from the faith, giving heed to deceiving spirits and doctrines of demons—1 Timothy 4:1.

And when they say to you, "Seek those who are mediums and wizards, who whisper and mutter," should not a people seek their God? Should they seek the dead on behalf of the living? To the law and to the testimony! If they do not speak according to this word, it is because there is no light in them—Isaiah 8:19,20.

Let us always weigh everything carefully against the written Word of God. To depart from God's standard is the quickest way to fall into error and deception.

This raises the question, "How can we know the source behind a spirit?" The answer can be found in the New Testament.

Beloved, do not believe every spirit, but test the spirits, whether they are of God; because many false prophets have gone out into the world—1 John 4:1.

The apostle John also gave the early church some specific instructions on trying the spirits:

By this you know the Spirit of God: Every spirit that confesses that Jesus Christ has come in the flesh is of God, and every spirit that does not confess that Jesus Christ has come in the flesh is not of God. And this is the spirit of the Antichrist, which you have heard was coming, and is now already in the world--1 John 4:2,3.

Every Christian should heed Jesus' warning for this day.

> "For false christs and false prophets will arise and
> show great signs and wonders, so as to deceive,
> if possible, even the elect"—Matthew 24:24.

In the current revival of the supernatural, we need to be very careful to check every miracle with the Word of God.

If we carelessly accept everything as coming from God, we will be easily deceived. A sign or a wonder does not necessarily come from God. It can come from Satan.

God has given discerning of spirits to the church, and I do not believe that He intended this gift to be used by the pastor only. This gift is for all children of God, although the pastor is sent by the Holy Spirit to administer the truths of the Spirit to the people.

Once in Erie, Pennsylvania, at a convention where I was speaking, a man stood up and shouted that a certain evangelist was a man of God and that the people should give heed to him. This he did three times, disturbing the meeting. Several men endeavored to quiet him, but he would not keep quiet.

I discerned that this was a demon at work and not the spirit of the man. I arose from my seat, discerning the evil spirit, and commanded it to be silent in the name of Jesus. This man caused no further disruption.

For the protection of the Church, pastor and layman alike must know how to discern evil spirits and how to deal with them.

Emotion or Anointing?

Anything goes in many churches. Hollywood evangelism thrives, and signs and wonders take place in large meetings without scriptural warrant or foundation, and the people are delighted and deluded! We need God's gift to discern spirits now more than ever.

Should we accept every supernatural event as coming from the Holy Spirit? Not everything that happens in a full gospel meeting is orchestrated by the Holy Spirit. As God increasingly manifests His power in the ministry of deliverance, Satan also steps up his lying signs and wonders. (See Matthew 24:24.)

When a person becomes born again and filled with the Holy Spirit, he may experience intense emotion. The degree of emotion is usually in proportion to the make-up of the person. A Scot might feel less emotion than a Frenchman, or a Pennsylvania Dutchman less than a Texan. The baptism in the Holy Spirit is not given to us to perpetuate feelings but to enable us to fight the devil in faith whether we feel good or not.

Unfortunately, Satan has been very clever in diverting thousands of Holy Spirit-baptized Christians into an orgy of feelings and emotions. The gospel owes nothing to the human emotions; it is based on faith in God's Word.

Many sincere Christians are deceived. When they manifest the gift of tongues or prophecy, they feel they must draw attention to themselves by waving their arms, jerking their bodies, or using falsetto voices in order to impress others with the "tremendous anointing of the Spirit" that they feel. All of these fleshly additions are unnecessary and are caused by the work of a deceiving spirit. The message may be of God, but the manifestation is of the flesh.

I remember casting a religious demon out of a lady who kept on crying "Hallelujah" in an unnaturally high voice. After the demon came out, she collapsed in a heap and couldn't utter a word. The church is swarming with religious demons today who are simulating holy things.

Not everything that happens in a pentecostal meeting is inspired by the Holy Spirit. Many occurrences are of the *human* spirit that has not been correctly disciplined. Other disturbances are the work of *evil* spirits who have taken control of the person.

What About Speaking in Tongues?

If the devil can simulate religious things, then speaking in tongues may not necessarily be a sign of the indwelling Holy Spirit! This presents a problem in the minds of many people, but I believe the answer is simple.

Long before God created man, the angelic beings that fell from their high estate in heaven were cast out to the earth with their leader, Satan. (See Revelation 12:7,8.) Imagine a demon gaining possession of a Chinese man centuries ago. That demon would learn to speak Chinese by indwelling that man. At the Chinese man's death, the demon would seek to inhabit another human body. This time he might enter an Indian and learn *his* language. Over the years, he might inhabit men and women of many different nationalities. In time he would learn all of their languages.

Imagine this multi-lingual demon entering an English-speaking man who came to one of our pentecostal churches. If he raised his hands and spoke in Chinese, Indian, French, or Hottentot, we would receive him without question! Many would say the man had been baptized in the Holy Spirit!

In a deliverance session held by the Reverend Lester Sumrall, a demon spoke perfect English through an ignorant girl who could not speak her own Philippine dialect properly. When the demon was cast out, the girl could not speak in English anymore.

In my own experience, when delivering people, I have heard demons actually sing and prophesy before being cast out. In such cases, the face of the person is usually contorted in horrible shapes, but the utterances can deceive.

Don't Be Gullible!

Where large crowds are gathered, religious demons love to "show off." Christians must not be gullible. Just because a person may fall down under the power of God, we shouldn't assume that all falling down is of God.

For instance, in the case of the demoniac son whom Jesus delivered, we read that "the spirit cried out, convulsed him greatly, and came out of him. And he became as one dead, so that many said, 'He is dead' " (Mark 9:26). Sometimes when an afflicted person comes into the presence of someone who casts out demons, the demon will throw them to the ground, convulse them, or cause some other physical manifestation.

I remember ministering to a girl in New York State who had just received a glorious baptism of the Spirit and had spoken in tongues. While magnifying God, her left arm oscillated violently, and we noticed this and inquired about it. A well-meaning bystander informed us that her tremors were caused by "the Holy Spirit," for every time she started to praise God her left arm started to oscillate.

We kindly pointed out that the Holy Spirit does not cause people's arms to oscillate violently like that. We then learned that this seventeen-year-old girl had epilepsy. In fact, her parents planned to have brain surgery performed on her when she reached the age of twenty-one. Doctors recommended such an operation to relieve the pressure on the left top side of the brain. In spite of this dire medical prognosis, I informed the people present that this girl needed deliverance.

As we began to constantly rebuke Satan's power, her arm started to oscillate violently. During the next fifteen minutes, the oscillation progressively decelerated. After thirty minutes, it ceased all movement.

We looked her in the eye and exclaimed, "Sister, we believe you are healed!" She started to weep for joy, telling us that the Lord had relieved all brain pressure. Later she testified in her own church of being healed by the power of God. No operation at the age of twenty-one was necessary. The demon had been cast out.

What Makes the Difference?

We underestimate the power of demonic forces. Demons try to keep us in ignorance, for we are not taught in our churches about these things. No matter how glorious your past experience has been, no matter how often you have spoken in tongues and prophesied, no matter how exemplary your life has been in the past, you can still backslide and permit a demon to gain a foothold in your life.

The gifts of the Spirit are gifts of God, but they will not prevent you from letting in other spirits. Once we have opened our lives to the spirit world, we must be careful that only the Holy Spirit possesses us, and that we are kept under the precious blood of Jesus.

Although Satan can speak in tongues through a person, everyone truly baptized in the Spirit can also speak in tongues as the Holy Spirit gives the utterance. (See Acts 2:4.) But how may we know the difference?

Jesus gave the answer: "You will know them by their fruits" (Matthew 7:16). If a tongues-speaking Christian does not manifest the fruit of the Spirit (see Galatians 5:22,23) in his life, he must be suspect in the assembly.

I believe that a pastor has God-given authority to insist that an unruly member keep silent in the church lest he give an utterance from an evil spirit or from his own human spirit instead of the Holy Spirit. And such an occurrence is altogether possible if a Christian does not walk in close fellowship with God.

This fact throws some light on the words of Jesus:

> "Many will say to Me in that day, 'Lord, Lord, have we not prophesied in Your name, cast out demons in Your name, and done many wonders in Your name?' And then I will declare to them, 'I never knew you; depart from Me, you who practice lawlessness!'—Matthew 7:22,23.

How could these people cast out devils, prophesy, and perform signs, wonders, and miracles? Surely, like Judas Iscariot, they must have been in right relationship with God at one time. But what happened to them? They yielded to pride, power, avarice, lust, and jealousy, and Jesus had no place for them in His kingdom. Tongues didn't save them; prophesying didn't save them. "You will know them by their fruits," said Jesus. (See Matthew 7:16.)

Paul focused on the balance between the fruit and the gifts of the Spirit in his epistles.

> Though I speak with the tongues of men and of angels, but have not love, I have become as sounding brass or a clanging cymbal. And though I have the gift of prophecy, and understand all mysteries and all knowledge, and though I have all faith, so that I could remove mountains, but have not love, I am nothing—1 Corinthians 13:1,2.

> Pursue love, and desire spiritual gifts—1 Corinthians 14:1.

Paul exhorted the Corinthians to seek both the fruits included in the all-embracing fruit of love, as well as the nine spiritual gifts mentioned in that same epistle.

The gifts without the fruit profit no one, including the user. Fruit without the gifts are beautiful, but lack power. We need nine gifts and nine fruit working in symmetry and harmony in this last-day revival of the supernatural.

3

How to Protect Yourself

One hot August day in Huntingdon Beach, California, I addressed a group of charismatic believers and preached on the ministry of Jesus in healing the sick and casting out demons. When I finished, I explained that Jesus wanted to touch people in the same way today. As I began to pray for people with various needs, many coughed, choked, and showed the usual manifestations of deliverance that happen each time I minister.

One Christian man suffered from a locked spine. He walked upright but had not been able to bend over for twenty years because his spine was "frozen." After explaining to him that his affliction was probably caused by a spirit of infirmity, I reminded him of the woman in the Bible who had a similar condition:

> And behold, there was a woman who had a spirit of infirmity eighteen years, and was bent over and could in no way raise herself up.
>
> But when Jesus saw her, He called her to Him and said to her, "Woman, you are loosed from your infirmity."

> And He laid His hands on her, and immediately
> she was made straight, and glorified God—Luke
> 13:11-13.

I emphasized that the woman's condition was caused by a demon—by a "spirit of infirmity." I then laid hands on the man, rebuked the spirit of infirmity, and commanded it to come out of his spine.

"Now," I said to the man, "just start bending your back, and keep on bending until you can touch your toes."

He looked at me somewhat startled. "I have not been able to do that for twenty years!"

But he acted in faith, and slowly but surely, each time he bent down, his fingertips stretched a little bit closer to his toes. After eight minutes, he started to shout. He had touched his toes! Jesus had healed twenty years of crippling in only eight minutes!

Continually Cleansed

Many Christians are offended by the idea that they might have a "spirit of infirmity" or be oppressed by some other demon. Some people get infuriated when we tell them that Satan may deceive them, visit sickness on them, entice them to backslide, or seduce them.

They reply, "Satan cannot bother me. I'm a Christian." We have met thousands who refuse to believe that Satan can worry, afflict, oppress, suppress, depress, frustrate, speak to, or lie to a child of God.

If Christians cannot be afflicted by Satan and his demonic hordes, why did several New Testament writers warn the early church about the enemy's deceptive tactics? We need to read these admonitions carefully and put them into practice in our daily lives:

> Nor give place to the devil—Ephesians 4:27.

Be sober, be vigilant; because your adversary the devil walks about like a roaring lion, seeking whom he may devour. Resist him, steadfast in the faith—1 Peter 5:8,9.

Resist the devil and he will flee from you—James 4:7.

The apostles Paul, Peter, and James addressed Holy Spirit-baptized Christians who had opened their lives, minds, and hearts to the Holy Spirit. Once they were empowered by the Holy Spirit, they could expect Satan to try to afflict or hinder them from doing God's will.

A Hole in the Hedge?

We are all familiar with the Book of Job. This righteous man, Job, had a nice, protective hedge around him. Satan used to prowl around this hedge day and night waiting for a hole to appear. And one day a hole *did* appear.

How did that happen? Job's fear tore down God's defenses. Remember what Job said? "For the thing I greatly feared has come upon me, and what I dreaded has happened to me" (Job 3:25).

God had not torn down the hedge. But Job had *created* a hole in the hedge *by his own fear.* God's protection could no longer operate because faith cannot exist where fear is present. Satan caused Job great distress and nearly destroyed his life.

Realizing these truths will help us to understand why some Christians get sick in body and mind. Why are some Christians in mental homes? This is not the fault of the gospel, for Jesus came to "preach deliverance to the captives" and to "set at liberty those who are oppressed" (Luke 4:18).

Whose fault is it that Christians succumb to physical and mental afflictions? Could it be that those who have received

Christ by faith begin to listen to the temptations of Satan and fall into his snare, thereby ignoring God's clear commands?

There is nothing automatic about salvation or any of the promises of God. They must be embraced by faith continually; we must resist the devil daily. If we do not, it is not God's fault that our protective hedge crumbles to give the destroyer access to our lives.

No Guarantees

The classic case of demon possession involves Judas Iscariot, whom Jesus had chosen as an apostle and disciple. It seems unthinkable that Jesus would have chosen a wicked man to heal the sick and cast out devils! Judas must have been sincere in his faith at one time, even as many in the church are today.

In John 13:2, we read of how Satan tempted Judas to do his foul deed:

> And supper being ended, the devil having already
> put it into the heart of Judas Iscariot, Simon's son,
> to betray him. . . .

The first act of the devil was to speak to Judas and *put the thought into his heart,* the innermost seat of his affections. Judas decided to obey Satan, and therefore turned his back on God and His Word. Judas, the disciple, was first oppressed, but finally he was possessed! "Now after the piece of bread, Satan *entered* him" (John 13:27).

If Judas Iscariot could end up being possessed of the devil, how much more can we today? Satan knows that his time is short, and he is working harder than ever to destroy the work of God that is transforming lives today. Being saved and filled with God's Spirit is not an automatic guarantee that you will continue in the faith.

Many sincere Christians maintain the unscriptural attitude that once they are born again and washed in the blood of Christ, Satan can never again touch them. Unfortunately, this teaching works in reverse and instead of providing protection makes many believers vulnerable to attack. Why? Because God's protection is not automatic!

Protected by the Blood

In the same way that a child needs to wash daily with soap and water, we need the continual cleansing of the blood of Christ. We do not take the Lord's supper once after conversion and then never come together to take it again, do we? Then why should we regard the cleansing of the blood of Christ in this way? We need continual cleansing. What do the Scriptures say?

> But if we walk in the light as He is in the light,
> we have fellowship with one another, and the
> blood of Jesus Christ His Son cleanses us from all
> sin—1 John 1:7.

Notice that "cleanses" is in the present tense. This means that it *continually* cleanses—not once in the past, but progressively now and in the future.

Every child of God must keep himself consciously covered and washed in the blood of Jesus Christ every moment of every day.

The blood of Jesus Christ is our greatest safeguard. Those involved in the ministry of deliverance should use the blood in faith to test all that they receive from the spiritual realm. Evil spirits are greatly agitated at the mention of the blood of Jesus.

A so-called Christian lady threw a real tantrum one day and rebuked me severely. But I determined that I was not going to be rebuked by a backslidden woman! I therefore commanded the demon to come out of her. It did—at least one of them did—and caught me by the throat and started to strangle me.

I cried, "The blood!" three times, and the demon went back into her.

But while it tried to choke me, the demon in the lady said, "There you are, *you* have a demon!" But it was a lie of Satan. And, through the blood, I overcame the demon.

On another occasion I experienced a demonic attack while I slept. In the middle of the night, I awoke to realize that the life had nearly been choked out of me. My heart was strongly oppressed. I felt as if life was almost gone.

I cried, "The blood!" three times. The demon departed rapidly, and the rest of the night was spent in peace. The next night at the same time, the same experience happened to my wife, and the same usage of the blood brought instant deliverance. No demon can get through the blood, but it has to be in place by faith.

A fellow minister told me the following story. He had gone down to the Bahama Islands to preach in a church. No pastor had ever been able to stay there because the unfriendly natives would come out from the bush beating their drums and shouting obscenities, which made worship impossible.

Our friend accepted the challenge and decided to claim that area for Christ. He walked around the perimeter of the church property, pleading the blood of Jesus aloud for Satan to hear and God to honor. Once was enough. Now there is peace. The disturbing evil spirit has departed, and a new missionary plans to take over the church. Now God's work will go on.

We do not speak enough of the blood of Jesus in our worship, our praying, and our attacks on Satan's strongholds. I am sure that if Christian assemblies everywhere would magnify the blood of Jesus, we would see carnal members stirred up and tremendous blessings poured out in new life for the church.

Power of the Blood

Medical science teaches that germs cause many sicknesses. Small parasitic creatures can breed in a portion of the body, multiply, and cause great distress. Other sicknesses, however, do not appear to be caused by germs.

Does God have some way of protecting His people from these germs? God is omnipotent, and nothing is beyond His power. Certainly, He can send His ministering spirits to protect us and to prevent evil spirits from putting germs into our bodies, if we pray for protection and keep God's laws.

Remember that nothing happens by "chance" or luck, but all is ordered by God. Germs are part of the curse that will be destroyed at the coming of Jesus Christ, and demons are merely agents in the hands of Satan to do his work at his bidding in the same way that soldiers obey their officers.

In our experience we have positively proved this fact. When boiling water spilled on a man's arm, we immediately prayed, acknowledging the power of the shed blood of Jesus Christ over the injury. Amazingly, no inflammation occured. This shows clearly that demons cannot visit the injured part of the body with germs when we recognize and use the blood of Jesus.

The same is true of cuts or scratches. We recently rebuked the flow of blood from a deep scratch in a child's forehead, and it immediately stopped. The wound was pinched together, and the next day the child was running around as if nothing had happened. The finest disinfectant in the world is the blood of Jesus Christ, applied by faith, because it keeps all unclean spirits away.

The only way we can protect ourselves from these terrible powers is by constantly keeping ourselves covered by faith in the blood of Jesus, which speaks defeat to these demon spirits. This is the blessed position of dwelling "in the secret place of the Most High" and abiding "under the shadow of the Almighty" (Psalm 91:1). We can trust no other protection or "shadow" than the covering of the precious blood of Jesus Christ.

Angelic Protection

God's angels also protect us from the small mishaps of life that are directly caused by demon spirits. Let's look at a tremendous promise in the Word of God:

> Because you have made the Lord, who is my refuge, even the Most High, your habitation, no evil shall befall you, nor shall any plague come near your dwelling; for He shall give His angels charge over you, to keep you in all your ways. They shall bear you up in their hands, lest you dash your foot against a stone—Psalm 91:9-12.

Isn't it wonderful to think that God's children, by faith in Jesus Christ, are the object of angelic care?

God's angels also bring answers to prayer. A spiritual battle in the heavens hindered the answer to Daniel's prayer and fasting.

> Then he [the angel] said to me, "Do not fear, Daniel, for from the first day that you set your heart to understand, and to humble yourself before your God, your words were heard; and I have come because of your words.
>
> But the prince of the kingdom of Persia withstood me twenty-one days; and behold, Michael, one of the chief princes, came to help me, for I had been left alone there with the kings of Persia—Daniel 10:12,13.

The demonic forces over that geographic area opposed God's messenger during the three weeks that Daniel fasted and prayed. When Michael joined the battle, the forces of God prevailed. Daniel finally received his answer.

Take Your Authority

Some of the experiences I've been describing may scare the timid soul from entering fully into his inheritance. But I would like to remind you that Jesus' promise still stands:

> "Behold, I give you the authority to trample on serpents and scorpions, and over all the power of the enemy, and nothing shall by any means hurt you"—Luke 10:19.

Satan's great weapon is fear. We must not succumb to dread or be paralyzed by fear. We must be bold in the strength of our Savior, who has told us to fear nothing. There is nothing to fear. Satan is a defeated foe.

Remember that some demons long ago said, "Jesus I know, and Paul I know; but who are you?" (Acts 19:15). Demons recognize that the man of God bears the same authority as Jesus—if he exercises the power and authority that Jesus has given him.

In Acts 1:8 we read that power comes upon us when we're filled with the Holy Spirit. Many people today are looking in vain for a demonstration of the power of God. No car goes forward until it is put into gear.

In like manner, no Holy Spirit filled Christian will produce any power until faith is exercised—until we determine that we are going to put an end to this evil oppression right now through Christ. Christians who take action get results.

The praying Christian who battles on his knees can attack the devil's stronghold with great effect. "Every place that the sole of your foot will tread upon I have given you . . ." (Joshua 1:3). We must place our foot on Satan's neck, take him by the tail, and cast him out.

What Should We Do?

The more a nation departs from God and His love as shown in Jesus Christ, the more that nation opens itself to control by demonic powers. This same principle holds true for individuals.

A drunken man opens himself to demon possession because of his lack of control. One who loses his temper is also similarly exposed. Unregenerate sick people who are weakened by suffering are also vulnerable unless someone prays for them by faith. And anyone who has anything to do with spiritism, occult sciences, or bloodless cults is almost certain to be affected.

How should we respond to the demonic forces that surround us? God's Word gives us the answer:

> Resist the devil and he will flee from you—James 4:7.

Resistance involves being on guard, being covered with the blood of Christ, and keeping ourselves under control.

The apostle Paul wrote about spiritual warfare being necessary to change situations in the natural realm.

> For we wrestle not against flesh and blood, but against principalities, against powers, against the rulers of the darkness of this age, against spiritual hosts of wickedness in the heavenly places— Ephesians 6:12.

These demon powers control the rulers of darkness and live in the first heaven of the earth's atmosphere. They do not live in heaven, for it was from there they were ejected.

The apostle Paul also listed the spiritual armor that Christians need to resist and fight the true enemy who opposes our interests on earth.

Therefore take up the whole armor of God, that you may be able to withstand in the evil day, and having done all, to stand. Stand therefore, having girded your waist with truth, having put on the breastplate of righteousness, and having shod your feet with the preparation of the gospel of peace; above all, taking the shield of faith with which you will be able to quench all the fiery darts of the wicked one. And take the helmet of salvation, and the sword of the Spirit, which is the word of God—Ephesians 6:13-18.

If we do not follow his advice, then we are exposed to demon powers and we must not blame God. He has made every provision for our protection.

4

Unique Demon Personalities

Demons have distinct and unique personalities just like human beings. No two demons are the same. I have witnessed very peculiar demonic personalities manifesting themselves through people.

I made an unusual discovery about demon personalities in Bogota, Colombia, South America. A Colombian pastor had asked me to go to the city hospital to pray for a lady who was dying. When we entered her hospital room, we saw a pathetic sight.

The woman was unconscious, and a rubber tube was inserted into her windpipe. She drew oxygen from a bottle, and her nose and mouth were taped shut. Her relatives had not left the room for four days. Hour by hour, they had stayed there weeping, which hardly charged the atmosphere with faith. The doctors informed me that she had but two hours to live.

I had been called to help, but what could I do? I hadn't the faintest idea, but I knelt by the bed and asked God to help me. Suddenly, an unearthly peace descended into that room—even all the relatives felt it. The Spirit of God enveloped us. I took the young lady's hand, laid my other hand on her forehead, and said, "Death, I rebuke you in Jesus' name." The next day I learned that the young lady had rapidly regained consciousness. Within one week she was released from the hospital.

The Colombian pastor who had accompanied me to the hospital was astonished by this good report. He asked me to meet with him in his office. With his head hanging, he admitted that he felt ashamed of his church because no one had been able to do this.

"Yes," I said, "but it was Jesus who healed her, not me."

"Yes," he replied, "but you *rebuked death*. I've never heard anyone do that before."

Jesus probably would have done the same in this situation because death is a spirit. This healing impacted the church in Colombia and opened them up to the working of the Holy Spirit among them.

Intelligent Beings

Remember that neither Satan nor his demon spirits are *things*. Neither should they be taken lightly. Demons are *beings* who possess malign intelligence, and each one desires to express himself through a body. A demon is not happy unless he has a body. Because they do not possess physical bodies of their own, demons seek to inhabit or use the bodies of humans or animals.

Many sicknesses are actually caused by demons, and they should be treated as such. Let's look at a scriptural example where this actually happened.

> Now He [Jesus] arose from the synagogue and entered Simon's house. But Simon's wife's mother was sick with a high fever, and they made request of Him concerning her. So He stood over her and rebuked the fever, and it left her. And immediately she arose and served them—Luke 4:38,39.

If this fever was only a physical problem, then how foolish to rebuke it! It makes no sense whatsoever to rebuke an inanimate thing. One can only rebuke something having intelligence, and Jesus knew that a spirit caused this fever. The fever left Peter's mother-in-law because it had to obey Jesus' authoritative command.

Calling the Enemy by Name

When you're engaged in spiritual warfare, it's important to know your enemy. The following evil spirits, demons, or devils are mentioned in the Scriptures. Each one is a personality, and the word used expresses their nature:

1. spirit of infirmity or weakness (Luke 13:11)
2. mute spirit (Mark 9:25)
3. dumb spirit (Mark 9:25)
4. distressing spirit (1 Samuel 16:14)
5. foul spirit (Revelation 18:2)
6. unclean spirit (Matthew 10:1)
7. spirit of divination (Acts 16:16)
8. spirit of bondage (Romans 8:15)
9. spirit of error (1 John 4:6)
10. spirit of the world (1 Corinthians 2:12)
11. deceiving spirits (1 Timothy 4:1)
12. jealous spirit (Numbers 5:14)
13. lying spirit (2 Chronicles 18:21)
14. familiar spirit (Deuteronomy 18:11, KJV)
15. spirit of the Anti-christ (1 John 4:3)
16. spirit of fear (2 Timothy 1:7)
17. perverse spirit (Isaiah 19:14)
18. sorrowful spirit (1 Samuel 1:15)
19. spirit of deep sleep (Isaiah 29:10)
20. spirit of harlotry (Hosea 4:12)
21. different spirit (2 Corinthians 11:4)

Satan, their undisputed overlord, exercises absolute control over his invisible hordes. His names reveal his variable characteristics:

1. Lucifer (Isaiah 14:12)
2. Prince of the power of the air (Ephesians 2:2)
3. Ruler of the demons (Matthew 12:24)
4. Destroyer (1 Corinthians 10:10)
5. Angel of light (2 Corinthians 11:14)
6. Serpent of old (Revelation 20:2)
7. Great dragon (Revelation 12:9)
8. Devil (Revelation 12:9)
9. Wicked one (Matthew 13:19)
10. Father of lies (John 8:44, KJV)
11. Murderer (John 8:44)

Is it any wonder that we are continually afflicted, frustrated, oppressed, perplexed, worried, and tormented by these disembodied beings? They swarm around us like mosquitoes. Once we are filled with the Holy Spirit and empowered to tear down the enemy's kingdom, we become special targets for their evil intentions.

Oppression and Depression

The most common form of attack is *oppression*. Oppression is a spiritual "pressing down" that leads to depression. If Christians tolerate this condition, then something worse may develop.

For instance, if we entertain an idea that is contrary to the Word of God, we become *obsessed* by that wrong idea or doctrine. Many false prophets today are demon obsessed.

Satan's goal in afflicting people with oppression, depression, or obsession is to lead them to a more dangerous state—*possession*. We must differentiate between possession of part of the body—as in epilepsy—and possession of the soul that leads to eternal separation from God. Even a Christian may end up in this latter kind of possession.

Many stubborn believers have disobeyed God for so many years that they have succumbed to demonic powers. In many cases, these tormented individuals need to be delivered by their pastors. Unspiritual members who yield to Satan's demons cause more trouble in local churches than we are willing to admit. Such people are probably only oppressed, but even oppression is a dangerous state in which to remain. A church split is always the work of a grinning demon.

Many years ago I tried the following approach on our two oldest boys who were quarreling. We rebuked this disturbing spirit and commanded it to stop troubling them. The boys instantly were released and stopped their disputing.

Confession Before Deliverance

No sin can be forgiven unless it is confessed and covered by the blood of Jesus. Scripture gives this stern admonition to all who return to the fleeting pleasures of sin:

> For if we sin willfully after we have received the knowledge of the truth, there no longer remains a sacrifice for sins, but a certain fearful expectation of judgment, and fiery indignation which will devour the adversaries—Hebrews 10:26,27.

Nothing will alter God's judgment unless that willful disobedience is confessed and put under the blood of Jesus.

I learned this lesson well in Caxton Hall, Westminster, London, England when an insane girl walked in to be prayed for. When her turn for ministry came, the friend who brought her explained that she had been taken from a mental institution in order to come to this meeting.

I did not inquire as to the type of insanity but laid my hands on the woman's head and started to rebuke the demon spirits. Nothing happened. I noticed that her face had the strained look of one in torment. The Spirit of God showed me that her trouble was caused by a persecution complex. This woman thought that everyone was against her and gossiped about her. When I confronted her with this revelation, she admitted that it was true.

I then explained that this was a sin that she must confess to God before she could expect to be delivered. She seemed quite surprised, but agreed, and prayed with me before the assembly, asking God to forgive her for thinking such ridiculous thoughts.

When I laid my hands on her head and prayed a second time, the spirit of insanity immediately left. Her face began to radiate with a bright smile of understanding and joy. I told her to turn around and face the congregation. A time of great rejoicing erupted as she praised the Lord for His healing power.

I learned an important principle from this case. People seeking release from bondage should ask God for forgiveness of their sins *before* we pray for deliverance. Confession must first be made unto salvation. Jesus cannot forgive us or deliver us until we say we are sorry. Stubbornness and pride have kept many people from receiving total freedom in Christ.

Freeing Finances

Can the enemy afflict believers with financial loss or poverty? We believe he can, but the following testimony demonstrates that God is greater than Satan in this realm, too. One of our church members owned a store, and above her business she rented a fine apartment. The owner was distressed because she could not rent it. As a result, she had lost over one thousand dollars. The Lord showed us that Satan was attempting to frustrate, impoverish, and withhold money from this fine Christian woman.

We visited the apartment with the owner, and together agreed for this restraining, evil power to leave. We pleaded the blood of Jesus in every room and cupboard and commanded the evil spirit to go. Then a word of prophecy declared that the apartment would be rented within a week. Within two days a tenant signed the lease.

The evil presence that had been cast out then descended into the store below, and business started falling off for no reason whatsoever. Adjusting price levels created no more business. Staff troubles, disputes, and unpleasantness added to the problems. Persistent, special prayer was made, and that malign spirit eventually left. Now both the apartment and the business are flourishing!

A Distracting Demon

Some of the demons I have encountered are so extraordinary that I hesitate to put the stories into print. The "music demon" is one such case.

During a stay with friends in Dunedin, Florida, I visited the wife of a member of the Full Gospel Businessmen's Fellowship. I asked her to explain her trouble. Everywhere she went, her head was filled with music. In fact, this phenomenon was so distracting that she could scarcely concentrate on what she was doing. Frankly, her plight amused me. What was wrong with a built-in radio playing all the time? I even asked her if it was classical music or rock and roll.

"No," she said, "it's not rock and roll, it's good music."

This puzzled me. If it had been rock and roll, I might have quickly said that the devil instigated her problem. But good music? What should I say?

Then she looked me squarely in the eye and said, "You're a man of God. Tell me, is it a demon?"

I was on the spot! This is one of those cases where you quickly pray, "Lord, show me! Lord, help me!" And as soon as I inquired of the Lord, the reply came back loud and clear.

"Yes," the Holy Spirit said, "this *is* a demon."

So I told the lady that it *was* a demon, but at this point I had no idea of its name. As we began to pray together, the Lord revealed to me that this was a *distracting demon*. As soon as I commanded this spirit to come out in Jesus' name, it coughed out, a most common form of ejection. In about one minute she was delivered of a distracting music spirit and has remained free since that day.

Binding Spirits of Murder

I encountered another demon personality in Dallas, Texas, at a meeting held by a Bible school. A certain woman came for prayer, and as usual, I asked, "What do you want from Jesus?" She replied that she was afraid of destroying herself and her three children. Satan's intention was to wipe out the whole family.

I then began to bind and command these murder demons to leave. I was not surprised when she began to scream in a loud voice, for I knew that Jesus had encountered this kind of demonic reaction many times. (See Luke 4:33,34.) It was not a pleasant experience. The demons manifested themselves in a frenzy of rage and then started to vomit out.

These murder demons were somewhat stronger than most of the demons with which we deal. Strong demons usually vomit out, often bringing mucus with them and sometimes even the poison that surrounds them. This is quite an operation! The very hand of Jesus, the Divine Physician, reaches right inside them and brings salvation and healing. I have seen many expensive operations done by Jesus for free, and the results are often left on the floor or in buckets. Gruesome and horrible, but true.

This deliverance took about half an hour. Then we began to pray for this woman to be baptized in the Holy Spirit. We taught her to plead the blood of Jesus out loud. Jesus gave her a new tongue, and she began to speak as the Spirit gave utterance. The vessel that had been filled with murder now overflowed with love. What a transformation!

The name of Jesus casts out every foul spirit, and the applied blood of Jesus cleanses the vessel. This paves the way for the Holy Spirit to come in and do His work.

These experiences taught me many lessons. We must not stop wrestling. We must never stop fighting. Many people receive prayer for deliverance but quit resisting when they do not get instant relief.

Christians should never stop resisting the devil for even a moment. We can cast him out of our lives, homes, offices, and factories. We are sons of God. We have been given dominion over every creature, including demons. We have dominion in the name of the Lord.

5

Deliverance That Lasts

Our first experience with deliverance happened in our Toronto church and involved a fine, converted, Catholic man who attended regularly. He had suffered from chronic asthma since birth and was also a heavy smoker. Although we prayed for him and anointed him with oil, he was no better. The asthma continued to plague him, and he could not quit smoking.

A woman suggested to me what seemed to be a preposterous idea. "Do you suppose this is a smoking demon?"

At that time, I had never heard of a smoking demon. Many Christians refuse to hear of them even today. If you had told me about an asthma demon, I wouldn't have believed it either. After all, wasn't asthma a nervous disease and smoking merely a dirty habit? Demon? Devil? Evil spirit? How could it be? The Spirit of God was leading and teaching me many things I could never have learned in Bible school!

First, I prayed with this man to receive everything from God, but he still remained bound. He had developed asthma as an infant and had not been able to work until he was twenty-six. For the next fourteen years he spent his hard-earned money on doctor bills, hoping to find a little relief.

I prayed with him, and he was marvelously baptized in the Holy Spirit with the evidence of speaking in tongues. Despite receiving this blessing from God, he was still afflicted with asthma and bound by nicotine.

Many Christians, who have been taught that the Holy Spirit will not enter an unclean vessel, refused to believe his experience. We learned that the Holy Spirit is given, like every other gift of God, on the basis of grace and faith— not because of our worthiness or holiness.

"Come Out!"

One day I said to this brother, "We think you may be afflicted by a smoking demon. How do you feel about having it cast out?"

He wasn't shocked at my suggestion that he needed deliverance. Because of his Roman Catholic background, he had learned to accept what the priest said as true. I suppose this is a great lesson for rebellious Protestants to learn!

Before praying, we led him to the church kitchen in the basement because we had read that demons sometimes come out crying with a loud voice. At that time, my wife and I had no first-hand experience in these matters, but we took precaution nonetheless.

My wife and I sat down, and our friend sat in front of us. I knew nothing except what Jesus had told me—and that is always enough! He had said, "In My name they will cast out demons" (Mark 16:17). I also remembered the teaching I had received about using the blood of Jesus in the presence of the destroyer.

We started to sing some choruses about the blood never losing its power. Then we launched an attack! "In the name of Jesus, come out!" As we gave persistent commands and pressed the battle hard, the demons of asthma and smoking started to cough out and vomit out.

After one hour and twenty minutes a huge pile of handkerchiefs soaked with sputum were on the floor. But our friend was gloriously healed! He stood up, inhaled deeply, and exclaimed, "Praise God! I am healed! I can breathe properly for the first time in my life!"

What had we done? As the apostle Paul said, "We do not wrestle against flesh and blood, but against principalities, against powers, against the rulers of the darkness of this age, against spiritual hosts of wickedness in the heavenly places" (Ephesians 6:12).

We cast out the spirit of infirmity that caused this man's asthma. Although asthma affects the breathing and nervous system, we learned that a demon could cause this affliction.

This brother is still healed today, and his heart was pronounced strong five years after the healing. He no longer needs to smoke because Jesus set him free. God uses him in the gift of tongues, interpretation, and prophecy in the assembly.

A Spirit of Suicide

Two days later, another man telephoned us. This Christian brother, who had been a deacon in a full gospel church, was battling a strong urge to commit suicide. Could it be that a Holy Spirit-baptized man—a deacon in a full gospel assembly—could be demon possessed?

What would our Bible schools say? What would the pastor of his church say? What would anyone say? Who cares what they say! I quickly told the afflicted man that demons were probably the source of his torment. Being desperate, he asked what he could do. Remembering the recent deliverance session where the asthmatic was gloriously set free, I felt I was ready for anything.

"There is one thing we can do," I said. "We can cast out these suicide demons."

"When?" he asked.

"Tonight," I replied, full of faith and the joy of the Lord! I was learning that I was seated in heavenly places in Christ and had been given authority over demonic forces.

My wife again came down into the basement kitchen with us. We sat on one side of the room, and this despondent man sat on the other side with his wife. The kitchen became an arena of spiritual conflict.

We began by singing choruses about the blood of Jesus because we didn't want these demons to attack us. There is nothing like a fresh reminder of the power of Jesus' blood. The demons knew they had no power over us. Then we gave the command.

To my astonishment, this man shot into the air about one foot off his chair. He landed with a thud, and his head shook to and fro as if he were a toy in a dog's mouth.

We doubled our forceful commands in the name of Jesus and ordered every foul suicide demon to come out. After one hour, many unclean spirits had come out moaning, coughing, vomiting, and writhing. Then they started to speak. We had read about demons who spoke to Jesus, but we didn't know anyone who heard demons speak today. We know differently now.

We asked the spirits how many more remained in our brother, and they replied, "Twenty." We counted them as they came out, paused at each fifth one, and asked again. Amazingly, they told the truth, although they argued and sometimes refused to answer. But our pressing commands in Jesus' name caused them to tell the truth.

"Fifteen." "Ten." "Five." The last demon put up a twenty minute fight, but the name of Jesus and an authoritative command expelled him. Finally set free from demonic bondage, this brother threw his head back and spoke in tongues, magnifying God.

He then made a pact with God; he said that if he was truly delivered, he would like God to give him the gift of prophecy. And the next Sunday around the communion table, this cleansed vessel brought forth a beautiful prophetic word that edified the entire church.

Sin No More

Such deliverances are spectacular. Seeing captives set free by the power of God exhilarates me. Manifesting Satan's defeat builds faith to tremendous heights. But deliverance is in no way automatic. Keeping your new freedom is dependent on maintaining a very close walk with God.

The apostle Paul simply wrote, "Work out your own salvation with fear and trembling" (Philippians 2:12). The apostle James tells us that "faith without works is dead" (James 2:26).

Some people who have been delivered in a most spectacular manner have returned to their old ways. Why the disheartening relapse? The demons have returned with a vengeance, and the outcome is usually worse than before. Epileptics have been gloriously delivered and released from their seizures. But because they did not walk more closely to the Lord than before, the demons returned.

We have ministered deliverance to people again when demons gain access to their lives through sin, rebellion, or simple carelessness. We must realize that demons entered into their lives only because of a previous weakness. Unless that gap is closed after deliverance, the same trouble will befall the person again.

Jesus warned a paralytic who had just been healed, "See, you have been made well. Sin no more, lest a worse thing come upon you" (John 5:14). Jesus indicated that his previous sin had caused his lameness. The remedy after deliverance was to sin no more. When we realize that the scriptural definition of sin is "the transgression of the law" (1 John 3:4, KJV), we are reminded that we can no longer do as we please. The walk with God after deliverance is very narrow.

Too many Christians have only a vague idea of what it means to follow Jesus. To them, He is a sentimental Lover with whom they can be as perverse as they feel inclined, and they think that Jesus will understand. They interpret being under grace but not under law as an excuse to do what pleases them, and they will not be tied to Scripture.

These careless, carnal Christians are likely to get sick and stay sick. "Sin no more, lest a worse thing come upon you" needs to be the text of all deliverance churches today.

"Is There Hope For Me?"

Perhaps the best scripture on this subject details the story of the man whose house was garnished, swept, and cleansed after the evil spirit had gone out. This demon was not so easily defeated. He wandered around, waiting for a convenient moment to return. Finally, the man backslid, and the demon *did* return and brought with him seven other spirits worse than himself. (See Matthew 12:43-45.)

To say that this man was not saved is to misuse the plain meaning of words. Obviously, he was saved, delivered, and cleansed in the blood; but he chose to backslide and consequently returned to his previous habit, and seven other demons came to plague him. The frightful possibility of such a relapse was made very real to me a number of years ago.

The telephone rang. "Is that you, Pastor Whyte?" The same man who had been delivered from twenty demons in our church kitchen seven years before was on the line.

"Yes," I replied. "What can I do for you?"

"Are you in the same place?"

"Yes."

"Do you still have the same ministry?"

"Yes."

He sighed with relief, saying that God had directed him to call me. He was trapped in the pit of sin again. "Do you think there's any hope for me?" he sighed. "I'm in a terrible mess."

I assured him that there was indeed hope, for the mercies of God are new every morning. So he came to my office.

His story was very sordid but a warning to us all. After his spectacular deliverance, he had moved out of the area and into the suburbs. The new church he attended did not believe the full gospel and did not teach or practice healing or deliverance.

One rainy day, as he drove downtown to his business in Toronto, he noticed a man at a bus stop. With compassion, he invited the man to get into his car. This worldly man offered our friend a cigarette. His offer opened a wonderful opportunity for our friend to witness about the salvation and deliverance available in Christ. But no. Instead, he took the cigarette, which proved to be his first step to hell on earth.

Each day he picked up this man, and each day they smoked. Soon they talked about drinking together. Their sin escalated from the tavern to the race track where they bet on the horses. Finally the new found friend said to our brother, "I love you."

As I listened to this man's story, I could hardly believe it. He had a beautiful wife, four wonderful children, and a good home. I had often visited them. What power drove a good Christian man to become a homosexual, leave his wife and family, and live in one room with another man? Psychology cannot explain this. It was the devil working through indwelling demons.

Worse Off Than Before

Theology explains that no Christian can have a demon. But I remembered how God had delivered this dear brother from a suicide demon seven years before. How could this Spirit-filled man have gotten a suicide demon in the first place? And what about the demons that were in him now?

I knew there was only one answer. He had arrived at this miserable state by disobeying the words of Scripture, "Do not . . . give place to the devil" (Ephesians 4:27). He had allowed the devil to occupy territory that had previously been occupied by the Holy Spirit.

The broken man slumped into a chair after his agonizing confession. He had scraped the bottom of the barrel of sin but was ready to be rescued again.

Without further delay, we gave the command. "Come out, in the name of Jesus!" The man was ready. The filthy demons began to pour out of him with almost continual coughing and choking. Without any asking on my part, they willingly named themselves as they came out. Lust, filth, uncleanness, perversion, cursing, etc. In twenty minutes he was completely free again.

When it was all over, I realized that I had seen a fulfillment of Jesus' words:

> "When an unclean spirit goes out of a man, he goes through dry places, seeking rest, and finds none. Then he says, 'I will return to my house from which I came.' And when he comes, he finds it empty, swept, and put in order. Then he goes and takes with him seven other spirits more wicked than himself, and they enter and dwell there; and the last state of that man is worse than the first"—Matthew 12:43-45.

This explained what had happened to the man. After his first deliverance, his "house" had been cleansed, swept, and put in order. But he had not kept it filled with the new Visitor, the Holy Spirit. His house had been left empty, so the suicide spirit came back. But he also beckoned to seven of his filthy friends, and they came in also. What a mess a Christian can get himself into by backsliding! But thank God, deliverance is available to all who bend the knee to Jesus and ask Him to forgive their sins and enter into their lives.

Seven years later, I met this same brother again in a certain church. Immediately I asked how he was doing. He joyfully told me that after his second deliverance, he returned home and made a full confession to his wife and family. They forgave him and took him back. God then began to prosper his business, and he bought a better home. Now he was keeping his house clean with the blood of Jesus, and the demon had permanently left.

How to Stay Delivered

God is restoring His power to the church to drive out demons, but the suffering person, whether a Christian or unbeliever, *must be willing to be delivered.*

Although moral perverts, alcoholics, and drug addicts say that they want deliverance, in their hearts they may want only temporary relief and not real deliverance to serve a living God. They are ashamed but unrepentant. Let me warn you that these *cannot* be delivered even if we spend hours with them. Many searching questions and discerning of spirits will be necessary.

Willing cooperation by the sufferer is of greatest importance in achieving a lasting deliverance. This is especially true with drug addicts and alcoholics. If they do not go on with God after the demons have been cast out, the demons will quickly come back. (See Matthew 12:43-45.)

This ministry does not rest on sentimentality. We may feel sympathetic for people, but unless they are willing, they cannot be helped. Even if we were to cast demons out of them (which is possible), these evil entities would only re-enter them when our back was turned.

People must be willing to be delivered and *stay* delivered. The hole in the hedge that gave Satan access must be closed after he has been cast out. We must refuse to succumb to the enemy's scare tactics. After deliverance we must live in close fellowship with God. Only then can we guarantee that deliverance will last.

6
Setting People Free

When this ministry began, I frequently spent from one-half to two hours in prayer for the oppressed. This became very exhausting and demanding on my time and strength. Over the years I began to see that deliverance could and should be speeded up. Quick and effective deliverance depended on two factors:

1. Our understanding of our powerful authority in Christ.
2. The willing collaboration of the one in need of deliverance.

In prayer we began to tell Satan that he was not going to stall. When we commanded him to come out *immediately,* he obeyed. Deliverances that previously took an hour now were completed in minutes. We began to pray for many afflicted individuals, and within minutes evil spirits came out coughing, choking, and screaming. Many people fell to the ground and then rose to their feet praising God, *free!*

I refused to talk to demons any more, nor did I encourage them to speak, or confess their names or presence. The Holy

Spirit showed me all I needed to know. Jesus commanded demons to be quiet and come out. This seemed to be the scriptural pattern. We did the same, and they obeyed. We learned that if we were uncertain, Satan and his demons took advantage of us, and put on a show by either refusing to come out or coming out only very slowly while we fought.

Every week in our church in Scarborough, a suburb of Toronto, Ontario, many came for release and the infilling of the Spirit. People who were afflicted with arthritis, heart troubles, lung troubles, and throat troubles sought and found healing with deliverance. Those who were bound by jealousy, anger, hatred, self-pity, murder, suicide, smoking, drinking, unlawful sex, and drugs were gloriously set free.

People with such problems came in a steady stream to us, and God, through our prayers, brought permanent deliverance to most of them. Immediately after their deliverance, we asked them if they would like the Holy Spirit to fill all the areas previously occupied by unclean spirits. Most agreed, whether they understood much or not, for they were hungry. In many cases, those who had no prior instruction on the baptism in the Holy Spirit began to speak in tongues much to their astonishment. What a change on their faces!

Thousands of afflicted and tormented people need this ministry in our churches today. Arguing whether these afflicted people are truly "saved" or not is pointless. They need help in whatever spiritual condition they find themselves in. God delivers today as He did in Jesus' day. The ministry of deliverance is meeting the deep spiritual needs of people like never before.

Defeated Demons

The apostle James tells us that "even the demons believe—and tremble!" (James 2:19). Christians need to understand their tremendous authority over demons in the name of Jesus. We should deal with them as defeated foes.

An unusual experience helped me to realize this truth. One day I was talking with another minister in our sanctuary. A drunk man unexpectedly lurched into the church and began to insult us. Realizing that I was face to face with a demon, I rebuked it in Jesus' name and commanded it to be subject to me. The results were extraordinary.

The man jumped up and down and cursed the name of Jesus. He pulled off his jacket and tossed it into the air. Then he tore off his shirt and threw it away, too. He dug his hands into his pockets, pulled out all his change, and scattered the coins all over the sanctuary. During his antics I continued to bind and rebuke Satan.

Next, the drunk staggered toward this minister and me and became quite contentious, arguing that he knew more about religion than we did. I continued to rebuke and bind the demons. Finally, he fell to the floor and started to spin like a top.

Suddenly the man stopped spinning, stood up, walked over to his shirt, put it on, and began to pick up his scattered coins. I helped him retrieve as many as I could. Then, after I had helped him on with his jacket, he sauntered out of the church very peacefully.

That instance dramatically demonstrated the power we have over demons. I knew that I would never again need to be afraid of anything or anybody. Jesus has given us practical protection against the powers of darkness that are continually arrayed against us.

Power Over Insanity

I witnessed another demonstration of this power over demons in dealing with a spirit of insanity. Mary had been oppressed by demonic forces and incarcerated in a mental hospital in Ontario. For part of each month, however, she returned to sanity. But with the approach of her menstrual cycle, she became violently insane.

Mary's mother, who was a Christian Scientist, took her daughter from the hospital for a few days each month but was warned to get her back to the hospital well before the next seizure.

When the mother heard about our ministry of casting out demons, she approached me to see if I could help. As a Christian Scientist, she knew nothing whatsoever about the ministry of deliverance. This woman's church taught that her daughter was not really sick—it was just "all in her mind."

Mary's mother arranged to bring her to the church office. She had apparently waited a little too long, however, for on the way to the church the mother realized that she was in a very dangerous predicament. Mary was losing her mind!

As soon as Mary got out of the car, she started shouting, "I'm not going in there!" Her mother tried to calm her, but Mary was furious. She turned and ran into traffic. Naturally, her mother was extremely disturbed, but I assured her that we could take dominion over this demon and command Mary to return. We did not phone the police; we called on Jesus instead. And sure enough, Mary returned in ten minutes. But she still refused to enter the church.

"Mary," I said in a stern voice, "I command you in the name of Jesus to go inside." And immediately she obeyed.

Once we were inside, I commanded her to enter the office. Then I commanded her to sit down. She was very obedient to every command. I was learning in a practical way that we do indeed have power over the enemy.

Her mother explained to me that Mary often became very violent and might try to push her hands through glass windows. Having been warned about this, I began to command these insane demons to come out of her. We engaged in a long battle, possibly because her mother was present and was not exercising real faith.

After about an hour, Mary uttered some terrible screams as some demons came out of her. At that point, however, other demons became greatly agitated. Mary rose to her feet, intending to push her hands through the glass windows. I remembered that a punch to the solar plexus would knock the wind out of a person temporarily. To stop her self-destructive behavior, I gave her a sharp blow in this area, and she immediately collapsed back into a chair and began screaming. I am neither recommending this treatment nor defending my actions, but in this case it worked.

Mary calmed down somewhat but obviously was out of her mind and still greatly agitated. It was now about 2:00 a.m. on Sunday morning, and we decided to take her back to the mental hospital.

"He'll never arrive," she growled. "I'll jab my cigarette in his neck while he is driving."

As we started, I again rebuked the spirits and commanded them to be silent. In a short time Mary fell asleep beside her mother in the back seat. My wife rode with me in the front seat and prayed continually. Soon, we safely returned her to the hospital.

The next day, Mary exhibited the worst spell of raging insanity she had ever had. For her own safety and the protection of others, orderlies placed her in a special padded room. Interestingly enough, Mary never suffered another attack after this one. The demons had yielded to our authority. The last we saw of Mary some years later, she was a counselor in a Billy Graham Crusade.

Delegated Authority

I was not surprised that the demons obeyed our commands. When Jesus sent out His twelve disciples, He commissioned them to "heal the sick, cleanse the lepers, raise the dead, cast out demons" (Matthew 10:8). Later Jesus also sent out seventy others two by two into every city and place where He intended to go. (See Luke 10:1.)

When they returned from their first missionary journey, the disciples exclaimed with joy, "Lord, even the demons

are subject to us *in Your name"* (Luke 10:17, italics added).
After hearing this good report, Jesus gave a wonderful promise to His disciples. In fact, this promise will strengthen any
believer who engages in warfare against the enemy:

> "Behold, I give you the authority to trample on
> serpents and scorpions, and over all the power of
> the enemy, and nothing shall by any means hurt
> you. Nevertheless do not rejoice in this, that the
> spirits are subject to you, but rather rejoice because
> your names are written in heaven"—Luke 10:19,20.

God's Word assures us that we can cast out demons in His
name, and they will not hurt us, for He has given us complete *power* or *authority* over all the power of the devil.

Cases of anemia, asthma, high blood pressure, colitis, and
heart trouble have positively been healed by commanding
the spirits of infirmity to leave the body, which they do with
open manifestations. Some even see "dark shadows" leave
them and feel a tremendous sense of relief.

Cartwheels in Church

One day a lady visited our church in Toronto. She had
heard our radio broadcast and was fascinated by the healing power of God in our midst. She suffered from degener-
ation of the spine, which would lead ultimately to being
confined to a wheel chair.

Because this woman was an accomplished swimmer and
swimming instructor, she was greatly concerned about the
outcome of her life. I took dominion over the destructive
spirit of infirmity that was at work in her spine, and immediately she received healing.

Quite understandably, this miracle of healing completely
changed her whole understanding of New Testament Christianity. This woman wanted to share her new-found faith

with her daughter who had severely injured her ankle doing gymnastics at school. The girl had been taking cortisone for some months to kill the pain, but her ankle hadn't improved.

One day Gail came to church, limping and carrying a cane. At the end of the service when everyone else had gone, she remained behind with her mother and shyly asked for prayer. Naturally, I agreed but was greatly surprised when she asked, "Can I do a hand spin after prayer?"

"Cartwheels in church?" I asked, laughing. "Why not, if Jesus is in the act!"

We laid hands on Gail and prayed in faith. Then, without further ado, she turned on her hands and feet *in church,* proving that Jesus had healed her. That experience completely changed her whole life, and she and her mother soon received the baptism in the Holy Spirit. Later on she was delivered from other emotional problems, and finally married my son Stephen. Gail graduated from the University of Toronto with a degree in physical education.

What a story! From my radio broadcast to a bride for my son. We never know what the Lord has in store for those who love Him.

Confession, Deliverance, and Healing

Another example of this power over demons concerns the mother-in-law of my oldest son. David married a fine Christian girl from Northern Ireland. Unfortunately, Genevieve's mother suffered from bursitis and ever-worsening arthritis in her right arm. In fact, she had been unable to raise her arm for three years. She knew nothing of divine deliverance, but Genevieve asked me to visit her and pray for her mother's debilitating condition.

I discovered that this kind Irish lady couldn't lift her arms very much. Even her hands were knotted and full of pain. She was able to get about only with much difficulty. Obviously, she would eventually be confined to a wheelchair if God didn't intervene.

I explained that my prayer would be different from that which she had previously known. I was not going to ask Jesus to heal her, but I would pray the way He told His disciples to pray. I also explained that in certain diseases, self-examination is often necessary to see if criticism, grumbling, or self-pity is a hindrance to healing. If these sins have taken root in the heart of an afflicted person, they must be confessed and forsaken. This she did.

Then she sat down, and I began to rebuke the binding spirits in Jesus' name. As I continued to take authority in the situation, she broke into a sweat and exclaimed, "I've never heard anyone pray like that before!"

I continued praying this way for about ten minutes. Sensing that a work of healing had begun, I told her to lift her arm above her head. She found this very painful, so I gently helped her, and together we got the arm up. The effort left her crying with pain and sweating profusely. Despite the difficult beginning, by the time I left her home she was able to raise her arm above her head. All the pain had left her hands, and she was able to move them freely.

What had happened? I had cast out a spirit of bondage that was binding her joints. This happens in hundreds of cases of arthritis. Now this lady testifies to everyone about the power of God and demonstrates her healing. Oh, the glorious liberty of the children of God! (See Romans 8:21.)

New Testament Patterns

The ministry of deliverance was quite obvious in the early church after Pentecost. Philip, the evangelist, was credited with working miracles.

> And the multitudes with one accord heeded the things spoken by Philip, hearing and seeing the miracles which he did. For unclean spirits, crying with a loud voice, came out of many who were

possessed; and many who were paralyzed and lame were healed—Acts 8:6,7.

Was there just one way to accomplish deliverance in the life of an afflicted person? No! God moved through the apostle Paul in ways that were previously unheard of:

Now God worked unusual miracles by the hands of Paul, so that even handkerchiefs or aprons were brought from his body to the sick, and the diseases left them and the evil spirits went out of them— Acts 19:11,12.

Other Scriptural examples exist, but we want to focus on *today*. The ministry of casting out evil spirits is a glorious reality *today*. We have witnessed many wonderful deliverances. People have been set free from suicide demons, epileptic demons, arthritic demons, cancer demons, insane demons, asthma demons, foul demons, sex demons, religious demons, and even spirits of fear and jealousy.

These have frequently come out crying with a loud voice, sometimes accompanied by vomitings, spittings, coughings, and writhings. Demons have argued back and refused to come out, but ultimately have obeyed the authority that God gives to His people. It is impossible to classify all these cases, but they all come out at the command of faith *in the name of the Lord Jesus.*

Deliverance is always certain, although it can be delayed and take a period of time. In fact, you may have to engage in more than one period of spiritual warfare before final deliverance is obtained for the victim. But victory is certain.

Set Free from Lust

One beautiful deliverance took place when my good friend, Dr. Russell Meade, of Chicago Bible College, brought a young college graduate for prayer.

This young man had a great need. Without going into unwholesome details, it is sufficient to say that he was bound by a spirit of lust. Naturally, I asked if he was married, and he replied that he was. Certainly, it would be a very unpleasant thing for a wife to have a husband bound by a lust spirit, and so I asked no more questions. I commanded the spirit of lust to come out in Jesus' name. Immediately, we saw the familiar choking ejection through the throat. After ten minutes all deliverance ceased, and by his countenance I knew he had been set free.

Some months later we met Dr. Meade in Chicago, and he referred to this young man. Apparently his wife had approached Dr. Meade and asked, "Where did you take my husband?"

"To Toronto," he said, "to Brother Whyte's church."

"Well, what did you do?" She inquired.

"We prayed for him," he replied.

"Well," she said, "I don't know what you did, but I would like you to know that I have a completely changed husband." A wife should know, shouldn't she?

Thousands are bound by a spirit of lust. This tormenting demon takes many beastly forms and shackles many with misery. But this is the day of the visitation of God's love. You *can* be delivered.

What About You?

If you believe that the Lord Jesus Christ was anointed to proclaim the "opening the prison to those who are bound" (Isaiah 61:1), we urge you to stand on Jesus' promise,

> "In My name they will cast out demons"—Mark 16:17.

Put away timidity and uncertainty, knowing that "nothing shall by any means hurt you" (Luke 10:19).

We must remember that the ministry of deliverance requires faith. Some experimenting, unbelieving Jews experienced disastrous results when they tried to cast out demons by using the name of Jesus without faith. (See Acts 19:13-16.)

Before beginning this ministry, cover yourself by faith in the precious blood of Jesus and keep under its shadow. Enter the battle with the full gospel armor. You don't need to shout at demons; they hear quite well and will obey you. Your faith will rise as never before as you behold the wonderful deliverances that can be wrought today in the mighty name of Jesus.

Part Two

Questions
and Answers

7

Demons and Deliverance

1. What is a demon?

The word *demon* comes from the Greek *daimon,* which means "an evil spirit." *Daimon,* in turn, comes from a root which means "a shadow." Satan, the supreme commander of all demons, sends these evil spirits upon people to bring shadows—darknesses—over the spirit of man.

Anyone who cannot believe in spirits will certainly have trouble believing in God. Beginning in Genesis, Scripture teaches that personal spirits exist. First, the Spirit of God Himself "moved upon the face of the waters" (Genesis 1:2, KJV). The same Spirit was breathed into lifeless Adam, and "man became a living being" (Genesis 2:7).

Many other references to the Spirit (or breath) of God refer to a *personal* Being. If the Spirit of God is a personal Being, then so are all other spirits.

Fallen Angels

Demons are actually fallen angels. One-third of all the angels were expelled from heaven because of the original rebellion of Satan against Jesus Christ. Let's examine the scriptural basis for their origin.

> And another sign appeared in heaven: behold, a great, fiery red dragon . . . drew a third of the stars [angels] of heaven and threw them to the earth—Revelation 12:3,4.

> And war broke out in heaven: Michael and his angels fought against the dragon; and the dragon and his angels fought, but they did not prevail, nor was a place found for them in heaven any longer. So the great dragon was cast out, that serpent of old, called the Devil and Satan, who deceives the whole world; he was cast to the earth, and his angels were cast out with him—Revelation 12:7-9.

The rebellious angels were cast down to the earth as disembodied spirits. And they are still here—whether we believe they are or not!

Certain liberal theologians have dismissed the reality of demons by the "accommodation theory." Since the common people superstitiously believed that demons caused sickness, Jesus "accommodated" Himself to their superstitions. Not wanting to upset them in their simplicity, He "went along with them," and cast out demons that really didn't exist! Anyone who believes the Bible to be the Word of God cannot possibly accept this theory.

Evangelical theologians generally accept biblical statements about Satan—although some of them fail to understand that Satan *maintains* his curse upon humanity through his hordes of demons. Satan finds this necessary because he is not omnipresent, as the Spirit of God is. But Satan has no shortage of help. The number of wicked, fallen spirits swarming on earth cannot be counted. They swarm like flies. In fact, the name *Beelzebub,* which is often applied to Satan, means "the lord of flies."

For the sake of simplicity, let us state that blessings come from God by His Holy Spirit, and cursings come from Satan by his unholy spirits. To fail to recognize demons is to fail to recognize the fundamental reason for the sufferings of humanity.

2. How does a person come under the influence of demons in the first place?

Demonic influence occurs in many ways. In certain cases, people have been born with demons. Years passed before I was persuaded by events and the Holy Spirit that an infant could be born with an evil spirit in him. Initially that thought seemed to be preposterous and revolting.

But so strong was the testimony of the Scriptures that the Lord is a jealous God, "visiting the iniquity of the fathers on the children to the third and fourth generation" (Exodus 20:5), that I began to look into the matter more closely.

I found many young babies who were extremely irritable and frequently wore out their mothers. Only when we prayed for them were they delivered. Babies and young children rarely have any noticeable reactions during deliverance. The demon probably has not sunk deeply into the personality of the child, and therefore yields easily to an authoritative command in the name of the Lord.

Demons may also enter young children. Many adults have testified that a terribly frightening experience as a young child gave opportunity for the evil spirit to come in. Having entered, the spirit will not leave readily, especially when a person waits fifty years before seeking deliverance.

During this period of time, the spirit digs in more and more tenaciously and may bring other symptoms such as fear, pains, arthritis, and stomach disorders. To prevent such demonic attacks in childhood, Christian parents should ask God's protection for their children each night and ask for a covering of the blood of Jesus.

Open to Oppression

Obviously, if a person gives place to the devil, as in drinking alcohol to excess or taking illicit drugs, a door may be opened for a wicked spirit to enter.

Any tampering with the occult—any "playful" experimentation with ouija boards, card playing, fortune telling, reading horoscopes, or the more obviously sinful practices of yoga, hypnotism, or spiritist seances, almost certainly exposes a person to demon oppression. Oppression, in turn, leads to obsession, and may ultimately lead to total possession and death. Those who seek deliverance should destroy all idols and occult literature in their homes.

Ephesus was filled with many idol worshipers who were converted through the preaching of the apostle Paul and the special miracles that God worked through him. How did these new believers forsake their former way of life?

> And many who had believed came confessing and telling their deeds. Also, many of those who had practiced magic brought their books together and burned them in the sight of all—Acts 19:18,19.

Avoid Backsliding

Some Christians open themselves to demonic attack by backsliding. If a Christian backslides or grows cold in his allegiance to Christ, Satan first tempts him to do wrong. If he sins, he opens himself for a spirit to enter and take control. The spirit doesn't come in immediately for God is very merciful. But if sin is continually indulged in and not forsaken after professed conversion, then such a person is wide open to demonic oppression in its many forms.

One classic case I dealt with many years ago involved a man who was delivered of suicide demons, which made a great noise as they came out. This man later backslid and became a homosexual. He returned to the Lord, weeping and confessing his sin; but by this time seven other spirits had entered in. (See Matthew 12:45.)

Once again he was completely delivered. The spirits named themselves without my asking them to do so. It was a real give-away of information on their part. Afterwards, this brother told me he had no power to stop these spirit voices speaking through him. But this time he was permanently delivered. This should be a very great lesson to all Christians to avoid backsliding.

3. How can you know when you have a demon?

Any person who is periodically attacked by a compulsion to act in a way that is contrary to his basic nature and alien to his own personality should suspect demon activity.

Whereas God visits mankind by His Spirit, Satan visits mankind by sending his demons. The result of such a demonic visitation is almost unbelievable. The object of attack demonstrates behavior that "can't be him." It isn't. Actually, the personality of the demon spirit manifests through him.

Such a person may be himself at times but sooner or later reverts to strange behavior that is totally uncharacteristic of him. Another name for this problem is "split personality," or *schizophrenia*. Seeing that schizophrenia could be caused by demonic interference was quite a revelation to me!

Spirits of infirmity may cause weakness or sickness in the human body. Spirits of lust incite people to commit adultery, homosexuality, or similar deviations.

Compulsive Behavior

Whatever the manifestation, knowing that we can actually bring pleasure to demon spirits by allowing them the use of our bodies for their own purposes should cause us considerable horror. What does Scripture say about our responsibility to consecrate our bodies to the Lord?

> Or do you not know that your body is the temple of the Holy Spirit who is in you, whom you have from God, and you are not your own? For you were bought with a price; therefore glorify God in your body and in your spirit, which are God's—1 Corinthians 6:19,20.

> For this is the will of God, your sanctification: that you should abstain from sexual immorality; that each of you should know how to possess his own vessel in sanctification and honor—1 Thessalonians 4:3,4.

If we are plagued by compulsive behavior or demonic oppression, we should confess our sins and submit ourselves to deliverance. Jesus came to break Satan's bondages and to proclaim release to captives. In the authority of His name, we can experience power over oppression.

4. What is deliverance?

Deliverance is the practice of expelling demons by an authoritative command in the name of Jesus. If you have a demon or suspect that you have one, I strongly recommend that you submit yourself to the ministry of deliverance. Ask a man or woman of God to cast the demon out in the name of Jesus Christ—after you have professed that Jesus Christ is your Savior and that you want to be rid of that particular evil spirit.

In general, the ministry of deliverance can best be explained as a forceful, commanding prayer given in the name of Jesus against sickness of spirit, mind, or body. Man is an inseparable trinity made up of body, soul, and spirit. If he is under attack in one area, he often feels the reaction in all three areas.

In the past, the church has generally confined itself to a simple prayer of petition, asking God, through His Son Jesus, to heal, restore, and deliver—and many wonderful answers have been granted; but many who received prayer were *not* delivered.

Who is to Cast Out Demons?

Did Jesus instruct His disciples to ask *Him* to cast out demons? Let's look at who was supposed to minister deliverance to the oppressed.

> These twelve Jesus sent out and commanded them, saying . . . "Heal the sick, cleanse the lepers, raise the dead, cast out demons. Freely you have received, freely give"—Matthew 10:5,8.

Jesus commanded *them* to heal the sick and cast out devils! They were expected to exercise their delegated authority in Christ.

Similarly, the apostle James instructed the elders of the churches to pray *over* the sick, not *for* the sick.

> Is anyone among you sick? Let him call for the elders of the church, and let them pray *over* him, anointing him with oil in the name of the Lord. And the prayer of faith will save the sick, and the Lord will raise him up—James 5:14,15, italics added.

The word "over" suggests that the one who prays *takes dominion over* the sickness and commands it to leave in the authority of Christ. The same kind of command is to be issued when we are dealing with demons. When this is done, the results that follow are often startling.

5. Can just anybody cast out demons?

No. Casting out demons is no parlor game for the curious. In fact, tangling with demons can be quite dangerous if you are not properly qualified.

What are the qualifications? Primarily, that you believe in Jesus Christ as your Lord and Savior and trust in His power. Jesus said, "These signs will follow *those who believe:* In My name they will cast out demons . . ." (Mark 16:17, italics added).

No human being has the power to cast out demons without Christ. Therefore, be very sure that Jesus Christ abides in you. If He is in you, you are more than a conqueror through His power and His name. (See Romans 8:37.) Any born-again Christian can cast out demons.

I am fully aware that the word "exorcist" has been used outside of Christian circles. Witch doctors often try to drive evil spirits out of people, but this must not be confused with Christian deliverance. No matter what a witch doctor might claim, he cannot cast out demons.

> "How can Satan cast out Satan? If a kingdom is divided against itself, that kingdom cannot stand. And if a house is divided against itself, that house cannot stand. And if Satan has risen up against himself, and is divided, he cannot stand, but has an end"—Mark 3:23-26.

No Other Power

Some spiritist mediums claim power to expel demons. This is impossible. Sometimes, though, they persuade the demon to go into temporary hiding, and the person who has been "exorcised" by a medium thinks that he has been set free. But, sooner or later, the demon manifests himself again, usually with worse effects than before. No other power drives out demons except the power of Jesus Christ.

What happens if someone who does not know Christ tries to cast out demons? Scripture records an incident where this actually happened.

> Then some of the itinerant Jewish exorcists took it upon themselves to call the name of the Lord Jesus over those who had evil spirits, saying, "We adjure you by the Jesus whom Paul preaches." Also there were seven sons of Sceva, a Jewish chief priest, who did so. And the evil spirit answered and said, "Jesus I know, and Paul I know, but who are you?"—Acts 19:13-15.

These Jewish exorcists had no personal faith in Jesus, but they had observed how the apostle Paul had successfully dealt with demons in the name of Jesus, so they thought they'd try it, too. What happened?

> Then the man in whom the evil spirit was leaped on them, overpowered them, and prevailed against them, so that they fled out of that house naked and wounded—Acts 19:16.

That's what can happen if you start playing at deliverance. But if you know Jesus Christ, you have nothing to fear. Take the authority that is yours, and cast out the demons in Jesus' name!

8

Demons and the Believer

1. Can a Christian be possessed by a demon?

The very phrasing of this question is unfortunate. The question is usually asked in a derogatory manner by those who totally reject the idea that a born-again Christian could ever be troubled or afflicted by a demon.

The problem revolves around the use of the word *possessed,* a word that suggests the demon totally inhabits and owns the sufferer with no area free and with free will absolutely blocked.

I do not believe a born-again Christian can be possessed by a demon. The very idea of a Christian who loves the Lord being *owned* and *controlled* by a demon is totally abhorrent and unacceptable. If Christians would abandon the use of this confusing word "possessed," and speak of demon problems in terms of "oppressions," "vexations," or "bindings," believers would avoid a lot of confusion.

The matter may be made even more clear by considering whether a Christian can be totally possessed of the Holy Spirit. From a theoretical point of view, we might be tempted to answer a hasty "yes" based on the following verse:

> Do you not know that your body is the temple
> of the Holy Spirit who is in you, whom you have
> from God, and you are not your own? For you
> were bought at a price—1 Corinthians 6:19,20.

In a certain sense we are the rightful property of the Holy
Spirit, yet even He can only *possess* us in practical terms as
we consciously *yield* ourselves to Him.

To speak of any Christian as being totally possessed by
the Holy Spirit implies that he is, at all times and in all places,
totally controlled by the Holy Spirit in all that he says and
does. But we know by experience that this is not so! Many
other factors enter in. The will of the person may cause him
to do something quite contrary to the known Word of God.

We must not make a Christian a puppet in the hands of
God. But suppose we fail to obey God? Is the Holy Spirit
then possessing us? He may be in us, but we are not giving
Him His rightful place at that moment of disobedience.

In like manner, a demon may trouble or afflict a Christian in any number of ways. But we are not suggesting for
a moment that such a Christian is "demon-possessed."

2. If not possessed, is there any other sense in which a Christian might "have" a demon?

Yes, certainly. But first, let us consider what we mean by
the word "have." What do we mean if we "have" a visitor
in our home (perhaps an unwelcome one)? What about "having" a mouse in our home or even a flea in our clothing?

We are not *possessed* by these visitors, but we may be
embarrassed by them. We may even be irritated by them and
try to get them out of our house or clothing as conveniently
as possible.

In like manner, Christians may receive unwelcome
demonic visitors. Take one of Jesus' disciples, for instance.
Peter started to rebuke the Son of God, no doubt with good

intentions, because he could not understand that Jesus *had* to be killed. Jesus replied to him in the same forceful manner as He had replied to Satan in the wilderness: "Get behind Me, Satan!" (Mark 8:33).

Peter meant well; he was sincere; but in trying to save Jesus from Calvary, he became an instrument of Satan at that moment. Was Peter "possessed of the devil"? Certainly not. But in his ignorance he gave *place* to the devil, who used his mind and voice.

Some might feel that Jesus was rather unloving by rebuking Peter, but His motive became quite clear when Jesus said to Peter,

> "Satan hath desired to *have* you, that he may sift
> you as wheat: but I have prayed for thee, that thy
> faith fail not"—Luke 22:31,32, KJV.

Satan was trying to "have" Peter, and when Peter gave place to him, Peter "had" Satan. If we entertain Satan in our thoughts or lives, we "have" him. Only as we expel him in the name of Jesus do we get rid of him and his terrible, gripping powers.

Jesus knew that Satan sifted Peter in the same manner that he had sifted Job many years before. The struggle became so intense that Peter, an apostle, openly denied his Lord before a young girl! Despite being a believer, he cursed and lied. Why did he cave in under stress? Because Satan attacked him and Peter gave place to him in his thoughts and words.

After Pentecost, Peter was a changed man. He had repented in bitter tears and learned to resist the devil. He was filled with the Holy Spirit.

Deceived and Devoured

Could it be that Satan tries to sift some of us? Why do some Christians feel constrained at times to curse God, or to destroy without reason, or even to murder or commit adultery? Many a person in a police court has said to the judge, "I don't know why I did it, but something made me." Who is the "something"?

The apostle Paul warned the Corinthian church "lest Satan should take advantage of us" (2 Corinthians 2:11)—and we must remember that the Corinthian church was made up of Spirit-filled Christians.

The apostle Paul also warned this church about the possibility of receiving "another spirit" (2 Corinthians 11:4, KJV). Obviously, then, Spirit-filled Christians *can* receive a spirit from Satan. Of course, this could happen only if they deliberately gave place to such a spirit.

The apostle Paul wrote,

> But I fear, lest somehow, as the serpent deceived Eve by his craftiness, so *your minds may be corrupted* from the simplicity that is in Christ—2 Corinthians 11:4, italics added.

Corruption of the mind of a Spirit-filled Christian can only be accomplished by demonic invasion. The corruption that comes from Beelzebub, the prince of decay, is implanted in the mind. "Mind corruption" in a Christian is a very serious matter, and a Christian who is under this kind of satanic attack is not helped by being told he "cannot have a demon." He needs counseling and the prayer of deliverance.

Worse than being corrupted is to be devoured by the enemy. Peter, who learned from his experience of being sifted, exhorted the early believers,

> Be sober, be vigilant; because your adversary the devil walks about like a roaring lion, seeking whom he may devour—1 Peter 5:8.

Peter didn't warn unbelievers—he wrote to Christian people. Satan is seeking to devour Spirit-filled Christians! What are we to say if he catches one, "eats" him up, and destroys him? Are we to run to our theological fortress of "once saved, always saved," or are we to understand that Satan *has* the Christian and has "eaten" him alive? This isn't a question of a believer having a demon; it's the other way around!

Seducing Spirits

The apostle Paul warns us "that in the latter times some shall depart from the faith, giving heed to seducing spirits, and doctrines of devils" (1 Timothy 4:1, KJV). Scripture indicates that a spirit can seduce a Christian.

If a man seduces another man's wife, and the once faithful spouse ceases to be faithful, she is obeying another spirit in committing adultery (which is also a spirit). Similarly, Satan may come as a charming personality and literally seduce a believer into spiritual adultery with demons.

If we do not control our fleshly nature and appetites, which are God-given, then Satan will tempt us to yield them to him. We are the ones who control the situation, not Satan. He has no power over one who keeps himself unspotted from the world, the flesh, and the devil. (See 1 John 5:18.)

Physical Afflictions

Sometimes, Christians may contact demons that cause terrible physical problems—such as epilepsy. No intelligent person would even suggest that epilepsy was from God, or that God ever intended that any of His children should suffer from such a terrible and embarrassing sickness. But we must not compound distress by suggesting that such a person is demon possessed. This will not help at all.

According to the Scriptures, these foul sicknesses are from Satan. We must recognize his influence in our fight of faith against all sicknesses of mind and body. When the sufferer manifests an attack of epilepsy or some other form of extraordinary behavior, we should recognize that a demon is exercising control upon a certain part of the body and needs to be dislodged by the prayer of deliverance given in Jesus' name.

One of the first persons to be delivered in our early ministry was a woman who had been experiencing attacks of nocturnal epilepsy. She has been healed ever since. This Christian woman had been dedicated to the Lord since childhood. She certainly was not *possessed* by a demon. After the commanding prayer of faith, the demon that was *vexing* her left, and she was permanently healed.

Yes, a Christian can "have" a demon, but he can also be set free if he confesses it to the Father and seeks his freedom in Christ.

3. Where does the Bible say that a Christian can have a demon?

People who ask such questions often demand that we show them exact chapter and verse to support our beliefs. Obviously, no quotation in the Bible says, "A Christian *can* have a demon." Neither will you be able to find an exact reference that says, "Thou shalt not smoke marijuana nor take cocaine!"

Actually, Christians in the Bible not only "had" demons, but also had them cast out. Scripture records the story of a woman who had been afflicted for years and was in need of deliverance.

> There was a woman who had a spirit of infirmity eighteen years, and was bent over and could in no way raise herself up. But when Jesus saw her, He called her to Him and said to her, "Woman, you are loosed from your infirmity." And He laid His hands on her, and immediately she was made straight and glorified God—Luke 13:11-13.

Jesus described this woman as "a daughter of Abraham" (verse 16), meaning she was a true believer. She was walking in the faith of Abraham. Scripture does not even hint that she was guilty of any particular sin. But she had been afflicted by a demon for eighteen years, even though she was a believer!

Forced into the Open

A Spirit-filled Greek Orthodox priest informed me that all new converts go through deliverance before being water baptized in his church. This is exactly what Justin Martyr, Polycarp, Clement, and Iranaeus—the early church fathers—tell us in their writings. All new converts automatically went through deliverance whether they asked for it or not. Church leaders dealt with spiritual contamination and filth before immersing new converts in water.

All those who come for deliverance in our meetings are professing Christians. Many have already been baptized in the Spirit. Although they praise God in tongues, bondages may still hinder their lives. In fact, I am inclined to believe that these demons are often brought to light *because* these people have been baptized in the Spirit. In other words, the presence of the Holy Spirit stirs up the other spirits that are in hiding. They are forced into the open by the Spirit of God where they can be dealt with and cast out in Jesus' name.

4. How could a demon and the Holy Spirit dwell in the same person at the same time?

This question is based on the assumption that "when Jesus comes in, Satan goes out." Certain holiness churches teach a "second work of grace," or "sanctification," which eradicates all traces of the sin nature in the believer.

Experience contradicts such an extreme doctrine, therefore we are forced to conclude that Christians frequently do things that are not consistent with the life of Christ *in* them. This does not mean that *every* willful act on the part of a believer is motivated by a demon; but many Christians *are* cruelly bound and need deliverance.

To say that such people are not believers is ridiculous. How many Christians are bound by habits? How many demonstrate temper and jealousy? Saying these people aren't Christians is easier than admitting believers can be troubled by evil spirits.

A well-known and respected minister in Toronto said that a Christian is like a hotel with many rooms. Only some of the rooms are surrendered, while others are still filled with spirits other than the Holy Spirit. Jesus only comes in where He is invited.

Some people take many months or years to realize all is not well in their lives; only after much inner turmoil have they reluctantly sought help. Although the Holy Spirit needed months to convince these people that rooms in their lives were still not filled with God, the prayer of faith brought immediate deliverance.

Upon conviction, they asked Jesus to come into those rooms—but Satan had to be expelled first, with their wills desiring it. We must be wary of a theoretical theology, lest we miss the blessing and remain bound.

Satan Filled Their Hearts

The case of Ananias and Sapphira is interesting. Few would dispute that they were members of the apostolic church in Jerusalem. This couple had witnessed great miracles and healings in the first century church. Yet Scripture records that they were influenced by demonic forces to be dishonest in their giving.

> But a certain man named Ananias, with Sapphira
> his wife, sold a possession. And he kept back part

of the proceeds, his wife also being aware of it, and brought a certain part and laid it at the apostles' feet.

But Peter said, "Ananias, *why has Satan filled your heart to lie to the Holy Spirit* and keep back part of the price of the land for yourself?"—Acts 5:1-3, italics added.

Even though they were Spirit-filled Christians, that did not prevent Satan from filling their hearts. The negative drove out the positive; the unholy drove out the holy; and they died as a result.

We have found by experience that many young people who have experimented with drugs and have been on psychedelic "highs" still suffered torment or mental bondage *after* receiving Jesus as Savior and *after* being baptized in the Holy Spirit. These troubled young people have come to us and asked for deliverance from this bondage. As soon as we have rebuked these tormenting spirits, the demons have responded by coming out.

In our churches today, there are many believers who need deliverance; but the church has not practiced this ministry. In our generation God is restoring the ministry of deliverance to set the oppressed free.

5. How can we be sure that any Christian's manifestation of the Holy Spirit is genuine, if Christians can have demons?

This question is often asked in particular reference to the manifestation of tongues. Suppose a Christian prays for the baptism in the Holy Spirit and then speaks in tongues. How do we know that this is a genuine working of the Holy Spirit? Couldn't it also be a demonic manifestation?

We need to remember the words of Jesus in reference to the Holy Spirit:

> If a son asks for bread from any father among
> you, will he give him a stone? Or if he asks for
> a fish, will he give him a serpent instead of a fish?
> Or if he asks for an egg, will he offer him a
> scorpion?
> If you then, being evil, know how to give good
> gifts to your children, how much more will your
> heavenly Father give the Holy Spirit to those who
> ask Him!—Luke 11:11-13.

Jesus clearly said that we need not fear getting something
we didn't ask for, or something evil. If you ask for bread,
you'll get bread. If you ask for an egg, you'll get an egg. If
you ask for the Holy Spirit, you'll get the Holy Spirit. No
one has ever asked the Father for the Holy Spirit and received
an *un*holy spirit. God is faithful and good, and He'll give
you what you ask for.

Do you think, then, that a Christian could earnestly ask
for the power of the Spirit and receive an unholy, devil-
inspired tongue? Certainly not!

I cannot emphasize too strongly the importance of the
blood of Jesus. What right have we to claim any of the blessings of Christ apart from the covering of His blood? The
person who asks for the baptism of the Spirit should also
say, "I plead the blood of Jesus." What other plea do we
have? How else can we presume to ask God for blessings
we don't deserve? But if you plead the blood, you can be
assured of protection from the deception of demons, and
you'll receive a genuine baptism in the Spirit.

By Their Fruits

We do find, however, that *some* people who receive the
baptism in the Spirit may still have a latent evil spirit in hiding, waiting to be cast out. The incoming of the Holy Spirit
may not always drive out the unwelcome spirits, although
demons do sometimes leave as the Holy Spirit enters.

In cases where demons remain in hiding, how are we to know when that Christian's "spiritual manifestations" are genuine? Very simply.

> "You will know them by their fruits. Do men gather grapes from thornbushes or figs from thistles? Even so, every good tree bears good fruit, but a bad tree bears bad fruit"—Matthew 7:16,17.

Similarly, the Holy Spirit brings forth holy fruit, but an evil spirit brings forth evil fruit.

If a particular manifestation is good and glorifies Christ, we may be assured that the Holy Spirit is in control.

6. Was the apostle Paul's thorn in the flesh a demon?

This question is a real hot potato! To many, the very thought that the apostle Paul could have "had a demon" is so revolting that it cannot be entertained. To get around this difficulty, many Bible teachers say that Paul had defective eyesight, caused by his ill treatment when he was stoned at Lystra. (See Acts 14:19.)

The difficulty is most easily resolved, it seems to me, by looking at the passage and accepting what it very plainly says.

> And lest I should be exalted above measure by the abundance of the revelations, a thorn in the flesh was given to me, *a messenger of Satan to buffet me,* lest I should be exalted above measure—2 Corinthians 12:7, italics added.

The grammatical construction in this passage is very interesting. Anyone who understands the most simple principles of English construction knows that the words in italics "a messenger of Satan to buffet me" are used *in apposition* to the words, "thorn in the flesh." In other words, the second expression explains the first. The apostle Paul explains his thorn in the flesh by saying it was "the messenger of Satan to buffet me."

The word "messenger" is a translation of the Greek word *aggelos,* which is usually translated "angel." Since demons are nothing more than fallen angels, we can conclude that Paul's thorn in the flesh was a demon who continually buffeted (struck, battered) him.

This "battering" is probably more literal than most people think. At Lystra, the apostle Paul was stoned until the people thought he was dead. Paul also describes his "batterings" in the following passage:

> In labors more abundant, in stripes above measure, in prisons more frequently, in [at the point of] deaths often. From the Jews five times I received forty stripes minus one.
>
> Three times I was beaten with rods; once was I stoned; three times I was shipwrecked; a night and a day I have been in the deep; in journeys often, in perils of waters, in perils of robbers, in perils of my own countrymen, in perils of the Gentiles, in perils in the city, in perils in the wilderness, in perils in the sea, in perils among false brethren; in weariness and toil, in sleeplessness often, in hunger and thirst, in fastings often, in cold and nakedness—2 Corinthians 11:23-27.

God permitted all these experiences of adversity because of the abundance of the revelations given to Paul, *to keep him humble.* The agent of this distress and woe was an angel of Satan—a powerful demon.

Have you ever wondered why things sometimes seem to go wrong when you are serving the Lord to the best of your ability? King David was hunted and persecuted despite his integrity and uprightness before God. How did David view his circumstances?

> Many are the afflictions of the righteous, but the
> Lord delivers him out of them all—Psalm 34:19.

Who sends these afflictions? Satan afflicted Job—but only with God's permission. Are we any different? Was Paul any exception?

Apparently, persecution is one kind of demonic oppression that no Christian can avoid. But we need not be depressed about it. Every Christian can claim an inner deliverance from demonic depression—Paul obviously had that kind of deliverance and was full of the joy of the Lord.

7. How can a Christian resist the demonic influences that surround him?

Resisting the enemy is both positional and practical. Scripture records that "he who has been born of God keeps himself, and the wicked one does not touch him" (1 John 5:18).

First, notice that the verse pertains to "he who has been born of God." By spiritual rebirth (as taught by Jesus in John 3:3-5 and John 1:12), a sinner becomes elevated to sonship in Jesus. He becomes an adopted son of God—a member of the royal family of heaven. His elder brother is Jesus, and all other born-again Christians are his brethren.

Second, we are told that this child of God "keeps himself." He accomplishes this by keeping himself clean and spotless from the world, thinking and practicing pure thoughts, and keeping himself under the blood of Jesus.

Then, providing he fulfills part two, he is in a position to rebuke the devil, resist him, and put him to flight. Not only can the wicked one not touch him, but Satan will flee from his presence, for he manifests the sweet savor of Christ. (See 2 Corinthians 2:15.)

Spiritually speaking, the believer smells like the Rose of Sharon and the Lily of the Valley. All his garments smell of myrrh and aloes and cassia. As Satan's "odor" is completely offensive to the Christian, in like manner the Christian's sweet "fragrance" is offensive to Satan; it reminds him of the total defeat he suffered when Jesus shed His blood on the cross to cleanse us from sin.

While the born-again Christian rejoices that "the wicked one does not touch him," let me quickly point out that this promise is conditional on his obedience. Some people try to hide behind this verse and claim that Satan cannot touch them or oppress them. Unfortunately, some Christians are professing (theologically) a freedom that they do not have in practical reality.

Are You Submitted to God?

Our churches are full of disobedient Christians whom Satan has cruelly bound. Submitting to deliverance to rid yourself of affliction or oppression is far better than acting as though bondage does not exist in your life. Once you are at peace on the inside, you will then be able to resist the demonic attacks that come to you from the outside.

James gives us an important key to resisting demonic influences. He says,

> Therefore submit to God. Resist the devil, and he will flee from you—James 4:7.

If your heart is not yielded to God, you will have difficulty resisting the enemy's temptations and oppression.

Peter had been sifted and used as a tool of Satan. What advice did he pass on to other believers who would face similar battles with such a cunning enemy?

> Humble yourselves under the mighty hand of God, that He may exalt you in due time . . .

> Be sober, be vigilant; because your adversary the
> devil walks about like a roaring lion, seeking
> whom he may devour. Resist him, steadfast in the
> faith—1 Peter 5:6,8,9.

If we first humble ourselves before God and then before our brothers and sisters in Christ, we are in a position of strength. Remember that God actively opposes the proud. (See 1 Peter 5:5.) Without humility, we will be quite unable to overcome Satan. We are warned that he desires to "devour" us—so we need to be careful to resist the devil with all our might.

While we have no strength of our own to fight the devil, we can claim the strength of Christ. We can say as the apostle Paul said, "I can do all things through Christ who strengthens me" (Philippians 4:13). With strength like that, the devil is a defeated foe!

8. How can you keep from giving a "place" to the devil?

First, recognize that you can have practically no resistance at all to demons without Jesus. The apostle Paul said, "I can do all things through Christ who strengthens me" (Philippians 4:13).

The natural man, without Christ, is spiritually weak and highly susceptible to infestation by demons. If Christ is not dwelling in him, a natural man can't do much about fighting off demons. If you do not know Christ, I urge you to turn from sin to Christ, and receive Him as your Lord and Savior. If you ask Him to come into your life, He will keep His promise and come in.

> "Behold, I stand at the door and knock. If any-
> one hears My voice and opens the door, I will
> come in to him"—Revelation 3:20.

But that is only the first step. Once you have received Christ and become a born-again Christian, then you must make it a habit to give no place to the devil. (See Ephesians 4:27.) You might as well face the fact that any part of your body can become a *place* for a demon. A demon will take anything he can get!

If we yield to our fleshly nature and give a hand, an eye, or an ear, a demon spirit with a particular characteristic may take hold of that particular part and occupy it. The spirit of lust may occupy the eye, for instance, and you may find yourself compelled to stare with lust at pornographic magazines or x-rated movies. The demon may compel you, even against your better judgment, to continue more and more in these practices.

One particular scriptural exhortation is certainly worthy of close attention.

> He who has been born of God [that is, the born-
> again Christian] keeps himself, and the wicked one
> does not touch him—1 John 5:18.

"Keeping ourselves" means steady abstinence from the wickedness of the world, continual walking in the Spirit, and keeping ourselves consciously under the blood of Christ.

By following the Holy Spirit, we can receive the strength to maintain continual fellowship with Jesus. Anybody who maintains that kind of fellowship with Him will certainly not give place to a demon!

9

Kinds of Demons

1. Are there demons that cause sickness?

Indeed there are. The real forces behind our physical world are spiritual in nature. God spoke matter into existence. He framed the worlds so that "the things which are seen were not made of things which are visible" (Hebrews 11:3). He created atoms and molecules. Our bodies are "fearfully and wonderfully made" (Psalm 139:14). Only when demonic forces invade our marvelous, God-created bodies are we afflicted with mental and physical sicknesses.

One passage of Scripture makes this especially clear.

> God anointed Jesus of Nazareth with the Holy
> Spirit and with power, who went about doing
> good and healing all who were oppressed by the
> devil, for God was with Him—Acts 10:38.

The word "oppressed" in Greek means "to overcome" or "to overpower" and suggests that the people healed by Jesus were set free from their sicknesses because an "overpowering" spirit left at the command of faith.

Look again. The verse says Jesus healed all that were oppressed (overcome) *by the devil.* In other words, Satan was the agent who caused their sicknesses. We must remember that Satan is the supreme commander of all demonic forces. As he gives the orders, his swarms of demons will invade, attack, and oppress human beings—and that includes afflicting us with sickness, disease, discouragement, depression, anxiety, and despair.

The Real Cause

The sick person, not understanding the cause of his condition, observes his symptoms and seeks medical treatment. I praise God for doctors, but Christians should understand that the real cause of some sickness is neither mental nor physical—it's spiritual. That's why Jesus rebuked the fever in Peter's mother-in-law. (See Luke 4:38,39.) As soon as the spirit behind the fever was expelled, the fever left and she was healed.

The chief objection to this teaching is the automatic revulsion that comes upon a Christian when someone suggests that a demon has invaded him and put a sickness on him. No one likes to hear bad news. Discovering we might have cancer or some other horrible disease is bad enough. But to be informed that we may have an infestation of invisible, living spirits in our body is so repulsive that we mentally reject it as being impossible. But rejection of the idea doesn't eject the demons!

I read of a missionary in South America who became so depressed that she left the mission field with chronic ill health. The Spirit of God finally revealed the cause of her problem: demons. She decided to fast. Every half hour she would kneel down, rebuke Satan and his demons, and claim victory. She continued doing this for one whole day. At the end of the day, she was totally delivered and restored to complete health.

2. When a person is sick, should you always cast out a demon?

God never planned for His people to be sick! In that sense, we can say that Satan is responsible for sickness. Who would think of blaming it on God?

Latent in the human body are natural recuperative powers. Tissue renews itself, and antibodies work to repulse the incursion of germs—but Satan is ever trying to prevent these processes. Prayer is very effective in these instances.

When any sickness persists over a period of time and does not respond to fervent prayer, we should consider casting out the binding spirit. This is true in cases of arthritis, bursitis, and other sicknesses of a similar nature. Constriction of the heart muscles, which we call angina of the heart, may well be caused by the activity of a binding spirit.

Are congenital defects always the result of sin? Scripture reveals God's perspective on just such an incident.

> Now as Jesus passed by, He saw a man who was blind from birth. And His disciples asked Him, saying, "Rabbi, who sinned, this man or his parents, that he was born blind?"
>
> Jesus answered, "Neither this man or his parents sinned, but that the works of God should be revealed in him"—John 9:1-3.

We are often asked to explain the case of the man born blind whom Jesus healed. The disciples assumed incorrectly that he or his parents must have sinned, but Jesus told them that the weakness existed so that He might reveal the healing power of God in restoring the man's sight.

We must not hide behind this story and believe that every congenital weakness or deformity is the will of God because it's not. The consequences of our forefathers' sins are still passed on to third and fourth generations. Neither can we say that the man "had a demon" because he was blind, but we *could* correctly say that Satan was the original cause of the blindness.

But even though Satan caused this man's condition, Jesus did not cast out a demon. He simply performed a creative miracle and gave the man his sight.

In like manner, when we are asked to pray for sick people, we do not always "cast out the devil." Instead, we often pray for a miracle, and God mercifully responds with astonishing signs and wonders.

3. If a person is set free from a demon that has caused sickness, should he immediately give up all medication?

The whole ministry of praying for the sick is very closely connected with the ministry of deliverance. Jesus "cast out the spirits with his word, and healed all that were sick" (Matthew 8:16, KJV). In many cases where people suffer from physical maladies, the spirit of infirmity behind the physical manifestation can be instantly cast out.

But even after deliverance removes the primary cause of infirmity, certain symptoms may remain. The pain and soreness may still be very evident, the inflammation may still be visible, the headaches and the actual germs or viruses may still be active.

If such is the case, what should the sufferer do? Should he give up all medication in evidence of his faith? Not necessarily—and certainly not without divine guidance in the matter.

Many have discovered, to their sorrow, the terrible results of plunging ahead without direction from God. In cases of diabetes, it would be pure presumption to give up taking insulin until the pancreas reverts to its normal insulin production.

Even after a healing, restoring the body tissues and read-justing to good health may require time. Taking medication during this period is not wrong, especially where viruses are still active. If the healing has been so extensive that medi-cation is not needed, that fact will soon become evident.

Some believers may find that an instantaneous healing removes all their symptoms. Others may experience a more progressive restoration to full health. In fact, this latter cir-cumstance is far more prevalent than the instantaneous miracle.

What About Taking Medicine?

Taking medication is not a sin. When Hezekiah was sick, he was healed—but apparently with the help of medication.

> Then Isaiah said, "Take a lump of figs." So they took and laid it on the boil, *and he recovered*—2 Kings 20:7, italics added.

Isaiah the prophet *ordered* this medication to draw out the poison from the boil.

Many would ask, "Why did Isaiah resort to medicine after he prayed?" Apparently because this was the revealed will of God in that situation. God told Isaiah to tell the king that He would heal him—but not without the fig remedy.

In some cases, such a procedure may be within the will of God for us today. The Word of God clearly states, "they [believers] will lay hands on the sick, and they will recover"(Mark 16:18). But this does not rule out the use of God-given medication. To refuse to take medication *can* be presumption, not faith.

Christians who scorn taking medication point to King Asa, who died because he went to the physicians. This is really a misstatement, for King Asa had been previously visited by the prophet Hanani, who rebuked him for trusting in his

Syrian allies, instead of trusting in the living God. King Asa was so enraged that he put Hanani in prison—hardly a suitable attitude for receiving healing from the Lord! (See 2 Chronicles 16.)

After Asa rejected the man of God, God rejected Asa. Like Saul who went to a witch for counsel, Asa went to his physicians for help and died. Had Asa been a godly man who received the prayers of Hanani and accepted his correction, he would no doubt have recovered whether he used the services of the medical profession or not.

Seeking help from doctors is not a sin. God has been good to give them an understanding about medicine, and there are many fine Christian doctors who can help us.

Whom Should We Seek?

I believe the proper procedure in cases of mental or physical sickness is clear. First, we are to seek God. Second, if the sickness persists, we ought to also seek the help of the medical profession. I do not recommend seeking a doctor and not seeking God in prayer.

In many cases, the prayer of faith with the laying on of hands *does* bring permanent and instantaneous healing and deliverance, and no further help or medication is necessary. But Jesus Himself said, "Those who are well have no need of a physician, but those who are sick" (Matthew 9:12). This seems to be a clear statement supporting the legitimate work of the medical profession, rather than a condemnation.

Many believers who take the extreme position of "no medication and no doctors" must reverse their stance in later years, when the body grows more frail. Some have died because they scorned all medication. Their refusal is not faith—otherwise they would not have died. At best, their extreme position is unwise enthusiasm bordering on presumption; at worst, it is plain fanaticism. God does not get the glory in cases like these.

Many natural curative drugs are found in the vegetation around us. Modern science will often manufacture these drugs synthetically instead of processing them from vegetation. Digitalis, for example, which comes from the foxglove plant, greatly strengthens weak hearts.

In recent years the connection between certain diseases and our lifestyles has come to light. We need to get enough sleep, exercise regularly, and eat a balanced diet. Using common sense and taking preventative measures can greatly reduce our incidence of illness and disease. If we do happen to get sick, we can come to God in faith for the healing He has provided through Jesus Christ.

Long experience has shown me that most people do not have as much faith as they think they have, or *should* have. They think they insult God by taking medicine. If you have been prayed for and you still carry symptoms, then by all means seek medical advice and get a prescription that can help you. Ultimately God is the One who will heal you anyway—if you believe.

4. Are there demons that cause emotional disturbances, or are such problems merely psychological?

We must understand that God wants to deal with us as whole people. Thinking of any problem as being psychological rather than spiritual is probably a mistake. It is more likely to be both!

Education has conditioned us to believe that a psychiatrist ought to be consulted for an emotional disturbance. To the humanist, the concept that the primary cause of blessing or cursing is spiritual makes no sense at all.

Doctors examine the body, psychiatrists probe the mind, and ministers deal with the spirit. But some professionals have noticed the relationship between these areas. Spiritual problems can bring on physical problems, and vice versa.

Unfortunately, many ministers work mostly in the intellectual realm, completely neglecting the spirit of man. The
church desperately needs men who are "spirit specialists,"
who can minister to the spiritual needs of the people. If the
spirit of man is oppressed by spirits of darkness, then his
mind will be dark, his emotions will be disturbed, and his
body may even become sick.

Intellectual men may call emotional problems by certain
psychological names and try to deal with them on the level
of the human mind; but the primary cause is often the operating of an evil spirit in the area of the human spirit, affecting both the emotions and the body.

Many negative emotions come from the working of evil
spirits. For instance, "God has not given us a *spirit* of fear,
but of power and of love and of a sound mind" (2 Timothy
1:7, italics added). Just as a spirit of fear can afflict a person
with terror or dread, the Holy Spirit can impart attributes
of power, love, and a sound mind.

5. Are there certain kinds of demons that may contaminate us through experimentation with the occult?

If a person plays with a skunk, he will most certainly end
up smelling like one! Occult involvement always contaminates the spirit.

If a person participates in a spiritist seance, inevitably that
person will absorb a measure of evil from the evil spirits
present. The Bible calls these spirits "familiar spirits" (Deuteronomy 18:11; 1 Samuel 28:7-19, KJV), because they are
the pet spirits who work through the medium. These spirits
are designated in the Scriptures as being foul or unclean.
As soon as such a spirit is contacted, and we act in a friendly
way toward it, we come under its malign influence.

Similarly, if we read horoscopes, play with ouija boards,
take part in levitation or table turning, or indulge in any form

of water or mineral divining, spiritual contamination begins. It is a spiritual law.

If a parent engages in any regular form of occult involvement, the children of the family may suffer as well. Recently, a British advertiser produced a billboard that showed a pregnant woman smoking. The advertisement warned that her unborn child would almost certainly be contaminated physically and mentally. In like manner, a pregnant woman who contaminates her mind by seeking after evil spirits will almost certainly bring some form of mental or physical contamination to her unborn child.

Spiritual contamination may lead to sickness, mental torments, and disgusting behavior patterns—especially those dealing with erotic sex, homosexuality, and general vulgar acts. Before we can experience deliverance from such bondage, we must confess our sins (even of ignorance), renounce them, and put them under the blood of Jesus. Then the prayer of command can cast out the contaminating demons.

History shows that when people depart from the Christian faith, the vacuum is filled up with other spirits. Heathen nations are full of demons and cruelty. When the Bible was banned from American schools, an open door was made for occult spirits to take over—and now most American high schools have at least one witch!

Our generation is experiencing a heightened interest in the occult. Unless God sends a true New Testament outpouring of the Holy Spirit, Satan will ultimately triumph and destroy many nations. The reverse is coming to pass, however, for God has promised to pour out His Holy Spirit upon all flesh—and that is happening today.

6. Are there demons that can come to us through our ancestors?

Yes, there are, but that's no reason for us to keep them forever! Deliverance is available for all congenital weaknesses that are caused by demons. Such problems generally fall into two categories:

1. Physical abnormalities caused by an unfortunate combination of genes.
2. Emotional or spiritual weaknesses received by heredity.

While we would not suggest that physical malformations or malfunctions are caused *directly* by demons, some emotional and spiritual weaknesses *can* be demonic in origin.

Unfortunately, the sins of the parents are often visited upon the children up to the third and fourth generations— that is, from eighty to one hundred years. (See Exodus 20:5.) The rebellion and disobedience of our forefathers are not our fault, but we carry the mental and spiritual scars nevertheless.

Infants of drug-taking mothers often die at birth, or they may need to be kept alive by a small dosage of some lesser drug because they have become addicted in the womb. Women who smoke can give birth to yellow-skinned babies who need a whiff of tobacco to soothe them and cause them to stop crying. They are already addicted. These babies have to be weaned from drugs at birth.

Venereal diseases can be transmitted through the bloodstream to unborn children, terribly affecting the eyes and other vital organs. A child can be born with a spirit of temper or a destroying spirit. The demon is literally *transmitted* from the woman to the unborn child while yet in the womb.

Many years ago, an experiment was carried out. The children of certain God-fearing parents were followed to see how they would fare in life. Their descendants became clergymen, lawyers, teachers, and people who made a positive contribution to society. Researchers also traced the children and grandchildren of a criminal family for comparison. Their descendants were found to be robbers, sex perverts, racketeers, and unemployables.

If your family history is less than exemplary, is this cause for despair? No! If you have been born with inherited demons, you can take heart in the knowledge that they can be cast out in Jesus' name!

7. Could there be such a thing as a "dormant demon" that might not manifest itself until a certain time in a person's life?

We believe that many children born of godless or rebellious parents—especially those who have indulged in forbidden occult practices—are already infested with demons. These demons may remain dormant or manifest themselves in strange behavior only at certain times.

I remember being told of a man who was prayed for in a church in northern Ontario. One of the spirits that was identified was named a "nicotine spirit." When challenged, this spirit was ejected through the throat, accompanied by a strong smell of tobacco. Amazingly, the man had never actually indulged in tobacco smoking!

How could this be? I believe he had a latent demon, which would have completely overpowered him had he given it the slightest toehold. But he resisted the temptation.

Let's look at a passage on temptation and sin.

> Blessed is the man who endures temptation; for when he has been proved, he will receive the crown of life which the Lord has promised to those who love Him.
>
> Let no man say when he is tempted, "I am tempted by God"; for God cannot be tempted by evil, nor does He Himself tempt anyone.
>
> But each one is tempted when he is drawn away by his own desires and enticed. Then, when desire

has conceived, it gives birth to sin; and sin, when
it is full-grown, brings forth death—James 1:12-15.

Notice what James says here. If one gives way to temptation, there is a *"conception"*—which means "the creation
of a new life." If a person has a latent demon, and he yields
to temptation, I believe this would actually cause a new
demonic life-activity in him—an activity which, like a fetus,
would grow, develop, and ultimately be born in that person's life.

The man who had the "nicotine spirit" within him had
never yielded to it. But if he had not resisted the temptation to smoke, the nicotine habit would have developed to
monster proportions.

A person having a latent spirit within him from birth may
be brought up in a disciplined Christian home and ultimately
make a decision to become a practicing Christian. He might
not discover this demon until many years later. But once discovered, a latent spirit can be cast out.

Even after a person has been delivered from a known,
recognized spirit, it may still be possible for other spirits
to remain hidden until the Holy Spirit brings them to the
surface. Then a second session of deliverance will be necessary. A commanding prayer in the name of Jesus can drive
the latent spirit out.

8. Are some demons stronger than others?

The Bible teaches that some demons have more authority
than others. If several spirits are binding a person, a "captain in charge" may lead the oppression. When delivering
a man from suicide, my wife and I had a strong feeling that
this demon was the "captain" who remained behind until
all the lesser ones were ejected.

Some people use the expression "ruler spirit." This expression is based on the following passage:

For we do not wrestle against flesh and blood, but against principalities, against powers, against the rulers of the darkness of this age, against spiritual hosts of wickedness in the heavenly places— Ephesians 6:12.

The categories of demons mentioned in this verse include:

1. principalities
2. powers
3. *rulers* of the darkness of this age
4. wickedness in heavenly places

There are two words in the Greek language for demons that rule nations. One is *daimon,* and the other is *daimonion.* The first word is usually associated with the powerful demons. The second word is a diminutive form denoting the lesser ranks. Those who teach about the existence of "ruler spirits" base their teaching on this passage in Ephesians.

Actually, that considerably weakens the teaching, since the context indicates that the authority of a "ruler spirit" extends to rulers, kings, despotic dictators, or governors. In other words, the work of a "ruler spirit" involves the actual *rule* of a nation or territory. Hitler or Stalin were no doubt controlled by such "ruler spirits."

While certain demons seem to be stronger than others, it probably is not wise to refer to any demon in the average person as a "ruler spirit." Maybe the thought would be more correct if believers used another word such as "captain" or "sergeant"!

Some teach that the one ministering deliverance must first challenge this "captain spirit" and cast him out, and then his minions will follow meekly after the boss has gone. We must remember, however, that some of these practices and methods were "discovered" in an actual dialogue with demons. Any information gained from demons should be open to serious question!

I do not recommend that we try to compel demons to speak and name themselves. Jesus commanded them, saying, "Be quiet, and come out of him!" (Mark 1:25). Demons are all liars and will use the most nonsensical statements in order to confuse the unwary and the novices in this ministry.

A demon, when challenged, might say, "I am the ruler spirit," thereby boasting of a rank that he does not have—and this statement could be enthusiastically received by those wanting to "prove" they have power to cast out a real, high-ranking demon.

I do not recommend forming doctrines based on the word of a lying spirit. I do not, as a general rule, hold any dialogue with these foul entities. I despise them and you should, too.

9. Is it safe to listen to what demons say?

Although some people who practice the ministry of deliverance often get into arguments with demons, I see no reason for this. Attempting a conversation with demons is neither good nor scriptural.

Once an evil spirit voluntarily told us the correct number of demons left in a despondent, suicidal man—and they were all successfully cast out. But we must remember that Satan is the father of lies, and his demons are liars, too. If you ask a demon to identify himself, or tell how he got into the person, his answer probably can't be trusted anyway. That's why you shouldn't talk to them.

Sometimes people will try to force a demon to tell the truth in the name of Jesus. But even then, demons find it almost impossible to tell the truth, and they will hedge and argue rather than tell the truth.

Furthermore, we are expressly commanded in the Bible not to communicate with evil spirits.

> There shall not be found among you anyone . . .
> who practices witchcraft, or a soothsayer, or one
> who interprets omens, or a sorcerer, or one who
> conjures spells, or a medium, or a spiritist, or one
> who calls up the dead. For all who do these things
> are an abomination to the Lord—Deuteronomy
> 18:10-12.

Scripture exhorts us to "resist the devil," not talk with him!
(See James 4:7.) Don't forget that King Saul lost his life by
disobeying God's law and seeking information from a
demon-possessed witch. (See 1 Samuel 28:7-19.)

The practice of seeking after those with familiar spirits
is condemned throughout the Scriptures.

> And when they say to you, "Seek those who are
> mediums and wizards, who whisper and mutter,"
> should not a people seek their God? Should they
> seek the dead on behalf of the living? To the law
> and to the testimony! If they do not speak accord-
> ing to this word, it is because there is no light in
> them—Isaiah 8:19,20.

Talking with demons is highly dangerous, even if you are
only arguing with them. Demons are completely unreasona-
ble anyway, and you'll never win the argument!

Our goal is to cast out demons quickly, giving no place
to them, and refusing to make any agreement with them at
all. We demand unconditional surrender. That is why Jesus
commanded the spirits to be silent and come out. If a spirit
can start arguing, he can delay his expulsion.

Whose voice do demons use?

We must remember that demons are invisible, spiritual
beings who have no physical organs of their own. They have
no voice box, no lips, no mouth.

Jesus made a revealing statement about the nature of demons.

> "When an unclean spirit goes out of a man, he goes through dry places, seeking rest, and finds none"—Matthew 12:43.

This verse seems to indicate that every demon craves expression through a physical body. When a demon cannot find a body to occupy, he is without rest. Demons of profanity and obscenity, for instance, crave human lips and voices so they can give expression to their blasphemous thoughts.

Most demons do not talk—but when they do, they simply use the natural vocal cords of the person whose voice they are controlling. Usually the tone is different, though—not the normally recognized tone of the individual involved—but a totally different kind of voice. But anyone can hear it.

After many years in the ministry of deliverance, we've found that demons do not speak very often. We simply ask the person about his need; after his confession of sin, we start commanding the demon to leave in the name of Jesus. As the spirit leaves, the person seeking deliverance may cough, sigh, or shake—but sometimes no outward manifestation occurs at all.

Occasionally, though, demons will argue with us, refuse to come out, or tell us to "shut up." In cases where demons want to talk, I do as Jesus did, Who commanded, "Be quiet, and come out of him!" (Mark 1:25).

10

The Ministry of Deliverance

1. Why must demons leave when a Christian gives the command?

Isn't it incredible that Jesus Christ shares His authority with *us*! We usually have no difficulty believing that *Jesus* has authority over evil spirits, but sometimes it is hard for us to grasp that He has now delegated that authority to us. Jesus said to His disciples,

> "All authority has been given to Me in heaven and on earth. Go therefore and make disciples of all the nations, baptizing them in the name of the Father and of the Son and of the Holy Spirit"— Matthew 28:18,19.

Somehow, that isn't quite the way we would expect Jesus to say it. We would more naturally expect Him to say, "All authority has been given to Me in heaven and on earth. *I* will go therefore . . ." But that isn't what He said. Rather, He said, "All power is given unto me . . . go *ye* therefore . . ."(KJV). Why did He say that? Because He had received power, and He has now delegated it to us.

If all demon spirits are subject to Jesus, then they are also subject to Jesus' people because we have His power. When Jesus died on the cross and shed His blood, He also stripped Satan and his demons of their power. Scripture says, "Having disarmed principalities and powers, He [Christ] made a public spectacle of them, triumphing over them in it" (Colossians 2:15).

We should not be surprised at this. Even before Calvary, Jesus gave His disciples power over demons—and it worked! They came back and reported, "Lord, even the demons are subject to us in Your name" (Luke 10:17).

In Jesus' Name

The name of Jesus carried great authority when He walked the earth, and today we are rightful bearers of His delegated authority. When we cast out demons in His name, we are doing it as His representatives. No demon can ignore the command of faith given by a child of God. He must obey, just as though Jesus Himself were speaking.

After the disciples had expressed their elation over discovering their newly found power over the enemy, Jesus said, "I saw Satan fall like lightning from heaven" (Luke 10:18). Apparently, Jesus saw the casting out of demons by His disciples as an indication that Satan was about to be defeated at Calvary and would fall as lightning to the earth.

Satan and his demons have no legal rights over a Christian. Demons must be absolutely subject to any Christian who knows and uses his authority.

2. Should inexperienced people try deliverance?

Anyone who tries anything new is obviously inexperienced, but experience comes by working at it. I was totally inexperienced when I began this ministry, and what I have learned has been learned the hard way.

How are we to become experienced unless we try? No one has ever done anything worthwhile in life without making mistakes. Jesus didn't tell His disciples to wait until they became experienced, or until they understood all the pitfalls. He told them to *do* it. They did it, and it worked.

The ministry of deliverance *does* attract a minority of very enthusiastic but immature people who rush in without quite knowing what is going on. Novices generally cause confusion without bringing deliverance. They may stir up the devil, but that's all.

Since more and more people are practicing the ministry of deliverance, and since some good books are available, I feel that newcomers should be encouraged to work with more experienced people. Novices should humble themselves under the instruction of the more experienced.

People who need deliverance often come to our prayer room following our Sunday evening service. I recently observed a situation where two newcomers came in and quite brazenly pushed aside a more experienced elder who was ministering to a young girl. After telling her that she had a "murder demon," they proceeded to "cast it out" and informed her that she might have killed someone someday if they had not had "discernment"!

Pride vs. Humility

Usually, all deliverance should begin with personal confession. The genuine gifts of the Spirit are not substitutes for personal confession and renunciation. If a suffering person comes to be freed from bondage, he (and not I) will express the particular need. I always encourage him to tell me, in the simplest language possible, what his need is— always remembering that confession is good for the soul.

Such sins as homosexual activity, adultery, and fornication need to be confessed, as well as "lesser sins." They need to be forsaken in prayer. Asking for God's forgiveness is a necessary prerequisite to receiving deliverance from bond-age. If the person feels too embarrassed to acknowledge his sins, he will not wholeheartedly enter into his deliverance. Confession is therapeutic.

The novice may find it more exciting to rely on the gifts of the Spirit to tell the person what is wrong. But when-ever we are ministering, we must be sure that we have the mind of the Spirit and not our own mind, which is quite frequently in error. All of us have heard sincere people say, "The Lord told me!" Among inexperienced people this is frequently not the Spirit of God but the mind of a proud person.

I remember an elder who announced that the Lord had revealed to him that his sister-in-law would die that very night. That was fifteen years ago. He himself died a few years later, but his sister-in-law is still alive!

I recently heard of another man who declared that God had revealed to him that he would not die until Jesus returned. He has been dead for ten years, and Jesus has not yet come back. What makes people say such things?

Experience Counts

To get back to our question—I think that inexperienced people should be permitted to enter into the ministry of deliverance, but they should also be willing to serve with the more experienced.

I find that the gifts of the Spirit do operate through me, but usually after I have begun to tackle a known, confessed problem. In the interest of safety, ask any others present if they have also had the same revelation in the Spirit.

Unfortunately, some evangelists have made capital out of their ministry by "putting a demon on" a person in order to "cast it out." The sufferer may have no knowledge what-soever of the "revelation," but in faith gratefully believes that he has been delivered of intended suicide, murder, or cancer, when in actual fact the whole idea came out of an enthusiastic (let's not say malicious) human mind.

Those inexperienced in the ministry of deliverance may get the demon stirred up into frenzied activity, but then they don't know how to use their authority to cast it out. Many times I've had to come to the rescue and command the demons to stop "acting up" and putting on a show.

Knowing how to handle strange manifestations comes only by experience. Novices should be encouraged to get that experience by working with mature, seasoned Christians who have been used in the ministry of deliverance.

3. Should any Christian attempt to cast demons out of others before he has been baptized in the Holy Spirit?

I am answering this question on the assumption that we are speaking of receiving the infilling of the Holy Spirit and manifesting it by the outflowing of glossolalia or "other tongues" from our innermost parts.

We must remember that the practice of deliverance is not peculiar to the days after Pentecost. Even the seventy disciples practiced this, much to their astonishment. (See Luke 10:1-20.) They were operating under Christ's delegated authority even though the Holy Spirit had not yet fallen on any of them!

Obviously, then, any born-again Christian can cast out demons. The great commission to the whole church begins with the statement that all believers should cast out demons.

> "These signs will follow those who believe: In My name they will cast out demons; they will speak with new tongues; they will take up serpents; and if they drink anything deadly, it will by no means hurt them; they will lay hands on the sick, and they will recover"—Mark 16:17,18.

The ministry of deliverance is not restricted to a select few, nor even to the Spirit-filled, but rather to every active member of the Body of Christ. Naturally, certain people will become leaders and teachers in deliverance and other ministries of the church.

I am not suggesting, though, that the baptism in the Spirit is unimportant. I believe that Jesus intended all New Testament believers to not only speak in tongues, but also to exercise the other gifts of the Spirit.

Working Miracles

The casting out of demons is equated with the gift of miracles in the following passage:

> Now John answered Him, saying, "Teacher, we saw someone who does not follow us casting out demons in Your name, and we forbade him because he does not follow us."
> But Jesus said, "Do not forbid him, for no one who *works a miracle* in My name can soon afterward speak evil of Me."—Mark 9:38,39, italics added.

Therefore any humble (and the more humble, the better!) believer *may* and *should* cast out demons, and thereby perform a miracle. If the born-again believer can perform such a miracle, then how much greater will the miracles be when he is Spirit-filled!

The church has been so weak and feeble that such plain teaching may cause dismay to many powerless church "leaders." They would rather not face up to the increased demonic activity of our day, instead retreating into theological formulas and dispensational nonsense. They reason that if miracles do not occur in their denomination, then they should not, or cannot, occur in others.

Any born-again Christian ought to desire all of God's power he can get. Not only should a believer be filled with the Spirit, but he should also be active in the ministry of casting out demons—not apart from the Body of Christ, but working under the guidance and direction of elders.

No one should ever tangle with this ministry unless he has a spiritual leader. No married woman should enter into this supernatural realm who does not acknowledge her husband as her head, or who does not attempt to have her children in subjection. Deliverance is a powerful ministry and needs people whose lives are in order and submitted to God.

4. Is fasting necessary for successful deliverance?

No, fasting is not necessary, but in certain circumstances it may be helpful. Let's examine a passage of scripture where an unsuccessful attempt at deliverance is mentioned with a lack of prayer and fasting.

> And when they had come to the multitude, a man came to Him, kneeling down to Him and saying, "Lord, have mercy on my son, for he is an epileptic and suffers severely; for he often falls into the fire and often into the water. So I brought him to Your disciples, but they could not cure him."
>
> . . . And Jesus rebuked the demon, and he came out of him; and the child was cured from that very hour. Then the disciples came to Jesus privately and said, "Why could we not cast him out?"
>
> So Jesus said to them, "Because of your unbelief; for assuredly, I say to you, if you have faith as a mustard seed, you will say to this mountain, 'Move from here to there,' and it will move; and nothing will be impossible for you. However, this kind does not go out *except by prayer and fasting.'*—Matthew 17:14-16, 18-21, italics added.

The King James Version describes this boy as being "lunatic." Whatever the modern medical term might be, the boy frequently fell into the fire or water. He may have been a spastic or subject to epileptic seizures. The disciples prayed to the best of their ability, but they lacked power to bring the needed results.

When Jesus "rebuked the devil," the demon that had caused his affliction departed from him. The disciples were very embarrassed and asked Jesus privately why they had not succeeded.

Fasting or Faith?

He replied that their unbelief caused their failure. They did not have the necessary faith for this deliverance. They were fearful. Most of us can react quite sympathetically to this. How many times have we had the same experience!

Jesus said that this kind of demon comes out only by "prayer and fasting" (verse 21). A more detailed account of the same story is given in Mark 9. Jesus did not cast out the demon until the father of the boy cried out, "Lord, I believe; help my unbelief" (Mark 9:24), showing that *someone* had to believe before the miracle was done.

This mention of fasting is one of the few cases in the Bible where a word may have been inserted by a copying monk in past centuries. He made the annotation, probably from his own thoughts, but later copyists put it into the text. In the minds of most Bible scholars, a real question hangs over verse 21.

If we dismiss verse 21, then we are driven to the conclusion that the real reason that the demon could not be cast out was their unbelief. To me, this seems more reasonable than to say that lack of fasting was the reason. If we were to go on a fast for everyone seeking deliverance today, we would have no time or strength left to pray for the multitudes of people who are now seeking help.

What's Our Motivation?

A few minutes before writing this, I spent an hour counseling and praying with an alcoholic. The demon of alcohol was visibly and definitely cast out of him. But I did not fast in preparation for this deliverance session. I had just eaten a light supper. I don't mean to discourage fasting. If a person is bound and in need of deliverance, it may be a good idea for *him* to have a mild fast, or to miss one or two meals before coming for prayer.

Fasting does not "twist God's arm," or earn deliverance from a "mean" God, but it *does* show the Lord the earnestness and seriousness with which the suppliant comes for healing. Fasting proves that the spirit of the man aspires to be stronger than the flesh. Denying the flesh also weakens the body against any resistance to the expulsion of the spirit behind the sickness.

Fasting was very popular among monks in the middle ages. This was a work of supererogation—or performing more than is required by duty or obligation. At the time of the Reformation, Martin Luther, together with hundreds of monks, left their cloistered solitude and gave up these practices, coming out into the freedom that Jesus gives us. The person who practices fasting is not bound by legalism, but our fasting should be led by the Spirit.

The disciples of Jesus were rebuked on one occasion for not fasting. Their freedom was contrasted with the Pharisees who fasted often while the disciples didn't fast at all! Obviously, this was a simple case of self-righteous criticism by the Pharisees! Jesus said they had no need to fast while they had the Bridegroom with them. We might ask ourselves the question, "Do we indeed have the Bridegroom with us?"

No doubt that fasting may be indicated in certain circumstances when someone is seeking deliverance. In general, however, there seems to be no need for the Christian to fast before praying for the bound and tormented.

5. Do Christians have authority to send demons to the pit of hell?

This is a very popular question, probably because Christians hope that the offending spirits can be confined to some kind of spiritual "garbage dump," so they'll not be troubled again! Many people have also asked where demons go when they are cast out. I'll try to answer both of these questions.

No passage of Scripture directs us to send demons back into the pit of hell. In fact, the opposite seems to be the case. In the story of the Gadarene demoniac, the demons begged to be sent into a nearby herd of swine because they feared that Jesus would torment them before their time. (See Matthew 8:28-34.)

We can infer that the ultimate torment for demons is to be cast into the pit, or "lowest hell." The demons knew that hell was prepared for "the devil and his angels" (Matthew 25:41), but as long as they were in the demoniac, they were safe from the pit. When the demons recognized Jesus, they feared meeting their ultimate destiny and requested the next best alternative—to go into the swine. The pigs plummeted over the precipice into the sea and drowned! The demons should have had more sense, but this proves how stupid they really are.

According to Scripture, the fate of Satan and his demons is sealed.

> And the devil, who deceived them, was cast into
> the lake of fire and brimstone where the beast and
> the false prophet are. And they will be tormented
> day and night forever and ever—Revelation 20:10.

Until this final act of Jesus, demons have a certain "legal" right to inhabit this planet. As long as they're here, they'll always be looking for the body of a man or beast as a vehicle to manifest their foul, evil natures. That's why demons inhabit the earth.

The earth has always been Satan's domain (even before he fell), and he still claims it as his kingdom. That's why, when Satan tempted Jesus, he showed Him all the kingdoms of the world in a moment of time and said,

> "All this authority I will give You, and their glory;
> *for this has been delivered to me, and I give it*
> *to whomever I wish"*—Luke 4:6, italics added.

The apostle Paul also refers to Satan as "the god of this world" (2 Corinthians 4:4, KJV).

The insane demons that left the Gadarene demoniac knew they faced a horrible fate, even if they were not immediately sent to the pit. Jesus taught His disciples what happened once an unclean spirit was cast out of a person.

> "When an unclean spirit goes out of a man, he
> goes through dry places, seeking rest; and find-
> ing none, he says, 'I will return to my house from
> which I came'—Luke 11:24.

Demons would be forced to wander around, seeking to re-enter the body from which they were ejected, or to inhabit another body.

Spirits, having been forced out of a body by the death of that person, have been known to cling to the building and haunt it. Family members and visitors may hear or see apparitions or sense their presence.

A Christian family moved into such a house in Oshawa, Ontario, some years ago, and the haunting spirits walked up and down the halls, opening and closing doors until the new owner called me to cast them out. This was done in about half an hour by audibly pleading the blood of Jesus in every room and closet, and then loudly commanding them to depart in Jesus' name—which they did. No more trouble was experienced.

Where do these demons go? Why, they just take off to find some other person to inhabit! As long as demons can live in a human being, they are happy; they will go to extreme measures to entice a person to sin. Satan tempted Judas Iscariot to sell Jesus for money, and later entered into him. First the temptation—then the overcoming of the person—who becomes bound until set free by prayer.

The whole strange teaching of "astral plains" taught among spiritists—the "seven stages" where departed humans go after death—is based on the fact that demons actually *do* stay close to this earth, perhaps in degrees or plains, but all "earth-bound."

This doctrine, believed so implicitly by necromancers (those who communicate with the dead), comes from demons. In the pit, demons will never again have human bodies in which to dwell and manifest themselves. Imagine a sex demon having no body to use in hell! That will *be* hell for the demon!

A human who was driven by this demon and never repented will face a horrible eternity.

> But the cowardly, unbelieving, abominable, mur-
> derers, sexually immoral, sorcerers, idolaters, and
> all liars *shall have their part* in the lake which
> burns with fire and brimstone, which is the sec-
> ond death—Revelation 21:8, italics added.

This place or pit was not prepared for humans, but for the devil and his angels. But if any human insists on permitting one of these foul spirits to govern his life, he will go *along with the demons* to the same place. Is it worth it?

Jesus offered forgiveness and deliverance to the tormented soul that fell at His feet. Christ set the Gadarene demoniac free to live in holy joy in this life and to enjoy the glories of heaven at death. He could have gone to hell, but he repented of his sins and his hideous condition. The demons will go to the pit, but not the demoniac. He is no longer bound by demons. He is a child of God forever.

6. What did the apostle Paul mean when he wrote, "God . . . will crush Satan under your feet shortly"? (Romans 16:20)

The word "shortly" means "with speed." The apostle Paul taught the Romans that they should expect to quickly tread on Satan's head, as David quickly beheaded Goliath after robbing him of his sword. Jesus, the fulfillment of David, took the terrible "sword" away from Satan (which speaks of his lying word), and put another "sword" in our mouth, which is the Word of God.

After the fall, God prophesied that the seed of the woman would bruise the serpent's head. (See Genesis 3:15.) The apostle Paul borrowed his metaphor from this ancient prophecy. All Christians may exercise their authority in Christ and put their feet on the neck of the defeated (but not yet dead) enemy, Satan, and render him powerless.

Not only did Jesus (the seed of the woman) bruise the head of Satan, but we, the continuing seed of the virgin bride (the church) are expected to bruise Satan's head by treading upon it daily in Jesus' name.

Christians ought to claim the following promise:

> You shall tread upon the lion and the cobra, the young lion and the serpent you shall trample under foot—Psalm 91:13.

So few have tried. No doubt the people in the church at Rome were also fearful, but the apostle Paul promised them that they would indeed trample Satan under their feet as a normal, daily exercise of faith.

Obviously, if Satan and his demons are safely under our feet, they cannot attack our minds or bodies. This is the only spiritually healthy stance for a Christian. Let us be careful lest, in our fearfulness or timidity, we depend on someone else to do the treading for us. There is no scriptural provision for this. Another Christian may cast a demon out of your life, but you must put your foot on him. If you do not, he may try to attack you again!

This is why Jesus admonished a man who had been healed of his paralysis, "Sin no more, lest a worse thing come upon you" (John 5:14).

The full meaning of Romans 16:20 is dramatized for us in Joshua 10, where the five kings who were determined to destroy the Gibeonites were themselves destroyed. Gibeon had seen the advancing Israelite army destroy Ai and Jericho, and so they wisely decided to throw in their lot with Israel and accept the leadership and protection of Joshua.

Later on, as Joshua moved forward quickly to defend the Gibeonites against the five kings, God sent hailstones to kill the armies of these kings. When the kings themselves saw that the battle was lost, they ran away and hid themselves in a cave, which was to become their tomb.

> So it was, when they brought out those kings to Joshua, that Joshua called for all the men of Israel, and said to the captains of the men of war who went with him, "Come near, put your feet on the necks of these kings." And they drew near and put their feet on their necks.
>
> Then Joshua said to them, "Do not be afraid, nor be dismayed; be strong and of good courage, for thus the Lord will do to all your enemies against whom you fight"—Joshua 10:24,25.

Then Joshua himself struck them and killed them, and hanged them on five trees. At sundown they cut them down from the trees, threw their bodies back into the cave, and blocked it up with heavy stones.

In the spiritual realm, God wants his children to face up to any demonic attack that might be launched against them—whether it be in the form of despair, shame, sickness, poverty, or famine. Demonic forces are constantly seeking to oppress us. We must never run from them, but face right up to them and put our feet squarely on the problem.

7. Shouldn't deliverance be done privately, away from the eyes of people who might not understand?

Obviously, the best way to deal with each individual would be to take them into a private room and counsel them. This also provides an opportunity to allow the Spirit of God to help us understand the problems of the sufferer. Following the time of counseling and listening to them, we can agree for the prayer of deliverance to take place. The evil spirits will soon be ejected, and whether they are noisy or quiet makes little difference.

Obviously, the actual and the ideal are often worlds apart. What should we do when confronted with a situation similar to the one that Philip faced?

> Then Philip went down to the city of Samaria and preached Christ to them. And the multitudes with one accord heeded the things spoken by Philip, hearing and seeing the miracles which he did. For unclean spirits, crying with a loud voice, came out of many who were possessed; and many who were paralyzed and lame were healed—Acts 8:5-7.

Philip was right out in the open air, and as he preached Christ to the people, the demons started to react very noisily.

What should he have done? Should he have taken them to a room in the City Hall? Should he have told them to keep quiet? Should he have taken each one aside for separate counseling and prayer? Obviously, this was not possible, and so it was necessary to have a mass deliverance service.

We are living in times when we may encounter such a great amount of demonic activity that there may be nothing else to do but stand by the microphone and publicly rebuke every alien spirit in the place, binding them and commanding them to come out. I have been in services where I have had to deal with hundreds of cases all at the same time.

I've met some people who think that this is a terrible thing to do in a public place—but what is our alternative when hundreds are seeking relief from oppression? In many places, it is not possible to deal with individuals privately because so many are seeking deliverance.

In our church in Scarborough, Ontario, we have tried to cope with this problem. The assistant pastor, the elders, and trained workers gather in our prayer room after the evening service. Some people receive counseling while others confess their needs privately. Then we lead them to renounce their sins and agree to put them away forever.

After this, we openly rebuke the demons in Jesus' name, while the workers gather around and pray in groups with each individual. I supervise and help in cases where difficulties may arise or where demons are stubborn and want to show off. People are delivered and filled with the Holy Spirit during these times of ministry each Sunday evening.

I know of no other way to avoid the possible confusion that might arise from a public deliverance service. If there are not trained workers, then we are compelled to handle the matter in whatever way we can. Deliverance is not an *extra* to the preaching of the gospel—deliverance is the very *center* of the gospel.

Jesus came that He might destroy the works of the devil and set the captives free. If people remain bound in our churches, then we are not fulfilling the great commission. Jesus said these signs shall follow those who believe in Him: "In My name they will cast out demons" (Mark 16:17).

8. Is it necessary to spend hours trying to set a person free from demons?

In our earlier experiences with deliverance, we were sometimes trapped by clever demons into spending much time and much energy, trying to budge the recalcitrant spirits. Some people have exhausted themselves by staying up all night but without bringing the sufferer to complete deliverance. Satan knows how to wear out the saints!

Sometimes, though, there are reasons for excessively long deliverance sessions. If a sufferer is seeking deliverance for wrong motives, we often find that the demons are hard to cast out. We must realize that demons claim a "legal right" to occupy a person who has given place to him and does not want to serve the Lord fully.

Someone may stir up a demon to great activity but fail to cast him out of a person. All we do is get him shaken *up* but not *out*. The demon may play with us and put on a show for hours so that we believe we are getting somewhere. When I encounter this situation, I immediately take charge, command the spirit to be silent, and order him to come out immediately. He usually does.

Ready and Willing?

Before beginning the prayer of deliverance, find out whether the one who is bound really wants to serve the Lord. Discover if any known sins are unconfessed. The sufferer should seek forgiveness for the sin or weakness that allowed the spirit to enter in the first place.

Long, drawn-out deliverance sessions are not scriptural. If I don't begin to get positive results within several minutes, I'll stop and inquire whether the person is sincere.

In one case, a woman informed my wife and me that she was a lesbian. We implored her to seek the Lord's forgiveness and forsake this sin, which is so highly condemned in

Scripture. To our astonishment, she admitted that she wasn't sure she could do it since she felt the experience was rather beautiful. This woman wanted to be set free from the stigma of her sin, but she didn't want to forsake it. No amount of prayer would have budged this unclean spirit. The demon had a right to stay there and manifest its unclean nature.

When a person is ready and willing, the time of prayer can be very exhilarating; but where unwillingness is present, it can drag the strength out of you because you are fighting an impossible battle.

We must remember, too, that more time may be required if a person has more than one demon. Even after a person has been delivered of one spirit, another may surface, and you may need to have a second or third session—or even more in some cases!

9. Must Christians force demons to name themselves before casting them out?

A more basic question needs to be asked, and that is, Can you trust demons to tell the truth anyway? If you must call a demon by name in order to expel him, the demon could stall a long time by giving you one false name after another.

I am aware that there are many sincere people who feel this is the right way to go about it. They do not attempt to cast out any demon until they first get its name. This idea is based on *one* incident in the life of Jesus: His encounter with the Gadarene demoniac.

The incident is related in three gospels, but it will be sufficient to look at Luke's version. After Jesus had commanded the unclean spirit to come out of the man, the next verse says, "Jesus asked him, saying, 'What is your name?' And he said, 'Legion,' because many demons had entered him" (Luke 8:30).

That *does* say that Jesus asked the name of the demon, doesn't it? But look again. I don't think it does. You'll notice that whenever Luke refers to the *man,* he uses the pronoun "he" or "him." Look closely at the following passage:

> When *he* [the man] saw Jesus, *he* cried out, fell down before Him, and with a loud voice said, "What have I to do with You, Jesus, the son of the Most High God? I beg You, do not torment me!"—Luke 8:28.

But when Luke refers to the *demons,* he uses the plural pronoun "they" or "them." Keep reading that same passage.

> And *they* [the demons] begged Him that He would not command *them* to go out into the abyss—Luke 8:31.

What should we conclude then? Why, simply, that when Jesus asked *him,* "What is your name?" He was asking the *man,* not the demons. And it was the *man* who said his name was Legion, for he apparently *knew* that he was full of demons!

Since no other place in the Bible instructs us to ask *anything* of demons, I conclude that we have no scriptural basis for asking demons to give their names.

In my own ministry, I have not found it necessary to get any kind of information from demons. Frequently, however, the Spirit of God will reveal by a word of knowledge the name and nature of the demon, and then we cast it out before it has any opportunity to lie.

10. Are demons always expelled through the mouth?

In the ministry of deliverance, a belief has arisen that demons must always be disgorged through the mouth. Apparently, this conclusion is based partly on the several cases of deliverance in the Bible where people cried out with loud voices, and partly on the experiences of people who have become nauseated during deliverance and have actually vomited out strange substances.

While many demons *are* cast out with these manifestations (and we are not to be alarmed if this takes place), yet experience shows that we can by no means expect that this will always happen. (I cannot imagine anyone actually *wanting* to see such things!)

With the increase of this ministry, we are learning to proceed with each case individually, with no preconceived notions about what will happen. Many demons leave with no visible manifestations at all—although in such cases, we usually get a strong inward witness that the demon has gone. The person involved also receives a deep peace, and their torment disappears.

I think we should do all that we can to stop any unpleasant demonic manifestations. Some are unavoidable, to be sure, but we certainly shouldn't encourage demons to make a show of themselves. Some people have mistakenly asked the demon to manifest himself. I tell him to be quiet and come out!

11. I've heard that there are sometimes unpleasant manifestations during deliverance. What are they? Are they necessary?

I want to guard against any teaching that would cause afflicted or tormented individuals to *expect* unpleasantness, and thus shy away from a greatly needed deliverance. If you are plagued by demons, let *nothing* hold you back from getting rid of that which troubles you! If the process turns out to be unpleasant or distasteful, just remember that hospital operations are also unpleasant—but often very necessary!

In my own ministry, I have been able to cast out demons with a minimum of unpleasantness. By binding the demon in the name of Jesus, and commanding the spirit to be quiet and come out, I usually see little outward manifestation.

But there are exceptions. In some cases, the person may tremble all over for a few seconds or longer; this is usually indicative of the demon's unwillingness to leave. In other cases, the person may fall to the floor.

This is what happened when a boy bound by a mute spirit was brought to Jesus.

> And when he saw Him, immediately the spirit convulsed him, and he fell on the ground and wallowed, foaming at the mouth—Mark 9:20.

Apparently the boy suffered from a case of epilepsy caused by demon oppression. Jesus rebuked this foul spirit, saying,

> "You deaf and dumb spirit, I command you, come out of him, and enter him no more"—Mark 9:25.

In other cases, the expelling of the demon may be evidenced by weeping, crying out, or even screaming.

> Then the spirit *cried out,* convulsed him greatly, and came out of him—Mark 9:26, italics added.

> But Jesus rebuked him [the unclean spirit], saying, "Be quiet and come out of him!" And when the unclean spirit had convulsed him and *cried out with a loud voice,* he came out of him—Mark 1:26, italics added.

Let no one think that he *must* cry or scream in order to receive deliverance, though. Such manifestations are caused by the departing demon, who certainly needs no help in expressing himself! But sometimes, in spite of the person's efforts to squelch unpleasantness, it happens anyway.

Occasionally, we encounter extreme cases where the departing demon causes violent coughing, nausea, or even vomiting. We must not draw back in astonishment or embarrassment from the one for whom we are praying if that happens. We must press on in our commands until the last spirit is expelled.

12. Why do some people experience only a partial deliverance when demons are expelled?

People are not totally delivered for several reasons. First, God delivers a person only up to the "ceiling" of his confession. If several demons are present and only one is confessed, then most likely only this demon will be ejected. As I pray for a person, the Holy Spirit often reveals another type of demon; when this demon is named and challenged, it will often react very suddenly and come out.

Sometimes people are not totally set free because they are not aware of all the areas in their lives that need deliverance. The Holy Spirit may gradually reveal their areas of need over a period of days or weeks. On the other hand, we can sometimes discover which demons are present through a word of knowledge.

Another reason why complete deliverance eludes some people is because their own faith is weak, or they may be quite unsure about this whole ministry anyway. Because of fear, they may not be fully cooperative.

If we succeed in dislodging a spirit after a strong fight, we then encourage the person to go home and ask God to reveal to them any other areas where they may be needing help. In this way, their own faith deepens, and they become more cooperative. Better results may occur in a second or third session than in the first one.

There may be any number of other reasons for partial deliverances. Sometimes, as we grow in grace, we find that latent weaknesses begin to show up more and more. A quick temper or jealousy, which has not troubled us very much in the past, may now begin to upset our Christian life. This has been my own experience, but when I asked for prayer, the spirit left me, never to return.

Submitting to One Another

Many of us may need to ask a brother or sister to pray for us. As we humble ourselves and submit ourselves one to another, God works mightily in our lives. Confessing our sin and asking for prayer may be very difficult, but humility may be the key to a more complete deliverance and healing. "Confess your trespasses to one another, and pray for one another, that you may be healed" (James 5:16).

If some well-meaning person approaches me and says, "Brother Whyte, the Lord has showed me that you have a spirit of ____ and need to be delivered," I do not brush him off as a "nut." I gladly submit myself, saying, "Very well, then you pray for me that I might be delivered." If his "discernment" is false (it may be caused by zeal without knowledge), then he will back off. But if his leading is from God, our spirits will witness to its truth. We should gladly submit to prayer.

At a meeting of charismatic ministers in 1973, a humble Episcopalian clergyman asked me to pray for his hasty temper. I took him aside, and we prayed together; he wept for joy as the evil spirit left him.

Submitting ourselves one to another knocks all pride out of us. God is looking for those with a humble and contrite spirit whom He can use to set others free from oppression.

13. If a Christian has been delivered of a demon, is there any guarantee that the demon will not return?

I think the answer to this question boils down to a matter of self-control. Unfortunately, many people who have experienced valid deliverances return to their old ways because of discouragement, pressure from relatives, or even business problems. The danger of backsliding after deliverance is very real, and if it takes place, the devil usually gains a much stronger foothold the second time.

This belief is supported by the following passage of Scripture:

> When an unclean spirit goes out of a man, he goes through dry places, seeking rest, and finds none. Then he says, "I will return to my house from which I came." And when he comes, he finds it empty, swept, and put in order.
>
> Then he goes and takes with him seven other spirits more wicked than himself, and they enter and dwell there; and the last state of that man is worse than the first—Matthew 12:43-45.

This teaching of Jesus should be sufficient motivation to keep all "cleaned up" Christians following hard after the Lord in their lives and their worship.

Peter also put it very plainly:

> For if, after they have escaped the pollutions of the world through the knowledge of the Lord and Savior Jesus Christ, they are again entangled in them *and overcome,* the latter end is worse for them than the beginning—2 Peter 2:20, italics added.

In verse 22, Peter likens this behavior to a dog returning to lick up its vomit. A revolting analogy!

In my ministry, I have encountered a number of people who have been delivered, only to return to their own ways. Ultimately, their problems became worse than they were before deliverance. We need to understand that temptation is very real, even after deliverance. But the devil is not stronger than Jesus. We do not have to give place to Satan.

Experience has taught me that at no time in my Christian experience am I in the final place of maturity and perfection. There is always room for more of Jesus; there are always deeper recesses in my spirit that need to be purged and invaded by the presence of Jesus. Because this is true, there is the ever-present possibility that demons may get control (or keep control) of some area of my life.

Keeping ourselves in the love of God, under the blood of Jesus, and unspotted from the world will prevent an evil spirit from returning. This was John's recommendation. (See 1 John 5:18.) Any born-again Christian can do this.

11

Objections to Deliverance

1. Isn't it dangerous to cast out demons?

Possibly. Driving a car on a modern highway can be dangerous if you ignore the rules!

We must remember that the kind of New Testament Christianity taught by the apostle Paul is not practiced in many of our churches today. Paul exhorted the early church to be soldiers, clad in protective armor, with a sword and a shield in their hands, battling against monstrous demon forces called principalities, powers, rulers of darkness, and wicked spirits.

> Finally, my brethren, be strong in the Lord and in the power of His might. Put on the whole armor of God, that you may be able to stand against the wiles of the devil—Ephesians 6:10,11.

> For though we walk in the flesh, we do not war according to the flesh. For the weapons of our warfare are not carnal but mighty in God for pulling down strongholds—2 Corinthians 10:3,4.

What resources for ordinary Christians! Why were these spiritual weapons necessary for the early believers? Because their enemies were powerful demon spirits controlling nations and organizations of men, evil spirits ruling in the dark places of the earth, and enormous numbers of evil spirits that attempted to harass them daily.

The Protection of the Blood

Is war dangerous? Only if you have improper equipment! If our armor is not worn properly, there will be chinks in it, and Satan will shoot his fiery darts through them. If we don't hold the shield of faith at the right angle, it will not avail. If we aren't familiar with the sword of the Spirit, which is the Word of God, then we have no offensive weapon. We are sitting ducks!

God has not only given us a protective armor that is impervious to Satan's attacks, but He has also given us the blood of His Son. I cannot recommend too strongly that those who enter into this battle deliberately cover themselves by faith in the blood of Jesus. Satan cannot get through the bloodline—but it is up to us to put it in place.

Before God released the children of Israel from Egyptian slavery, the blood of lambs had to be sprinkled on the lintels and sideposts of all Israelite homes before the angel of death passed over. If no blood had been used, death would have come to the first-born in every family. (See Exodus 12.)

Obviously, Satan will launch a counterattack when you become a nuisance to him. But it is better to go in and win than to sit on the sidelines and lose. The best form of defense is attack. That is why Jesus tells us,

> "Behold, I give you the authority to trample on serpents and scorpions, and over all the power of the enemy, and nothing shall by any means hurt you"—Luke 10:19.

What About Laying on of Hands?

There has been a very common objection to the laying on of hands in connection with deliverance. Many have said that we should not put our hands on anyone with an evil spirit, lest it enter *us!*

This may have some basis in common sense, especially in cases where the sufferer is oppressed to the point of insanity and violence. But I do not believe there is any danger of a "kick-back" from the demon or that the wicked spirit can get into us through the laying on of hands. The power of the Holy Spirit in us is infinitely greater than the power of Satan.

I usually begin deliverance sessions by praying for the person without laying my hands on them. If the sufferer begins to show signs of distress, I then use the laying on of hands to bring the force of the Holy Spirit to bear upon him. I often think of this as being similar to connecting a battery charger to the terminals of a dead battery. The power of the Holy Spirit flows into the demon-oppressed person and helps to drive out the evil spirit.

If you are inexperienced and uncertain about the whole matter of deliverance, then I suggest that you keep your hands off. Better wait until you've gained some experience.

To those who battle under the blood without fear, there is absolutely no danger. Satan and his demons are in danger. Jesus conquered them all at Calvary. With millions of people waiting to be delivered, let us arise, put our armor on, and begin to make war against Satan.

2. Shouldn't we just preach the gospel and not concern ourselves with the ministry of deliverance?

This is a favorite question with those who do not understand. The Bible says that Israel limited God by their unbelief:

> They turned back and tempted God, and *limited*
> the Holy One of Israel—Psalm 78:41, italics added.

They believed as much about God as was convenient for them in their way of life. Many of these people fill both the pulpit and the pews of our churches today. To them, the gospel of salvation is *limited* to John 3:16.

Now I am certainly not objecting to sermons preached on John 3:16! Every sinner needs to be born again and believe on the Lord Jesus Christ for salvation. But the church has been commissioned to do more than preach John 3:16. What instructions were given along with the great commission?

> "Go into the world and preach the gospel to every creature. He who believes and is baptized will be saved; but he who does not believe will be condemned.
> "And these signs shall follow those who believe: In My name they will *cast out demons;* they will *speak with new tongues* . . . they will *lay their hands on the sick* and they will recover"—Mark 16:15-18, italics added.

Jesus equipped His twelve disciples and later the seventy with much more than a simple gospel proclamation when He sent them out.

> Then He called His twelve disciples together and gave them power and authority over all demons, and to cure diseases. He sent them to preach the kingdom of God and to heal the sick—Luke 9:1,2.

> After these things the Lord appointed seventy others also, and sent them two by two before His face into every city and place where He Himself was about to go. . . . Then the seventy returned

with joy, saying, "Lord, even the demons are subject to us in Your name"—Luke 10:1,17.

Christ delegated complete authority to His followers to
cast out demons. This is the first sign that Jesus mentioned
that would be given to prove the authenticity of genuine
Christianity.

Philip the evangelist, because he did not preach a limited
Christ, saw God confirm His word with signs following.

> Then Philip went down to the city of Samaria and
> preached Christ to them. And the multitudes with
> one accord heeded the things spoken by Philip,
> hearing and seeing the miracles which he did. For
> unclean spirits, crying with a loud voice, came out
> of many who were possessed; and many who were
> paralyzed and lame were healed—Acts 8:5-7.

If a clergyman minimizes any part of the plan of salvation, he undersells his congregation on the meaning of salvation. In New Testament Greek, *salvation* means "to be
made whole" or "to be delivered." The salvation of the Lord
means soundness for man's spirit, soul, and body.

Preaching the Full Gospel

I once spoke on a Toronto radio station about the miracles of lengthening legs and straightening twisted spines that
God had performed in our midst. After hearing how God
miraculously touched specific cases, an inspired listener
wrote about having a crooked spine and one leg shorter than
the other. He decided to come to our church, and said he
had faith that our prayers would cure his condition.

I was on the spot! Should I have kept my mouth shut?
Was I treading on dangerous ground?

When the man showed up in church one Sunday and later went to the prayer room, I knew the "moment of truth" had come! Asking him to sit in a chair, I held his two legs and discovered that his right leg was five-eighths of an inch shorter than his left leg. I prayed and asked Jesus to heal the man. Immediately, the right leg grew out before our eyes until it matched the left one, and his spine became straight!

He wrote several days later, saying he had tried every test he could think of and the miracle held firm. He later returned to have a spirit of fear cast out. The man was gloriously healed and set free! I was glad that I had a *full* gospel to present to that man!

Should we leave out any part of the good news of salvation? Should we have the joy of seeing sins forgiven, but put up with being afflicted with physical sickness and mental torment? I admit that not everyone we pray for is healed or delivered—and there may be many reasons why—but that is no reason for failing to preach a *whole* gospel.

Debating With Skeptics

During a TV appearance in Toronto, I appeared side-by-side with a liberal, unbelieving minister. He thought that the first eleven chapters of Genesis were pure myth, and he didn't believe in demons at all.

I explained that the Bible spoke clearly about demons and how Jesus dealt with them by casting them out. I showed how Satan entered into Judas Iscariot and how the disciples also cast out demons. This liberal minister replied that demons were the "interpretations" of the men who wrote the gospels and the book of Acts. He wanted proof.

I told him about people who had been bound in mind or body and who were permanently set free when we cast out the demons in Jesus' name. What further proof did he need? Then I asked the liberal minister what came out of these afflicted people when they cried or fell to the ground.

His reply was surprising. "I have no doubt that you healed them!" he remarked. I corrected him and pointed out that I was only an instrument in the hands of Jesus. How could people receive miraculous healings and deliverance if demons do not exist? He had no answer.

Today Jesus is restoring all the gifts and offices of the Holy Spirit that the church might preach a whole gospel as Philip did. As we walk in faith and obedience, we can expect the same experiences and results to follow our preaching.

Remember, casting out demons is at the top of the list of signs that should follow our preaching. (See Mark 16:17.) Deliverance is not something we can sweep under our theological rug and forget. God is restoring the ministry of deliverance as an essential part of the gospel to be carried to all nations.

3. Isn't it mentally unhealthy to become too "demon conscious"?

Those who are engaged in the ministry of deliverance are often accused of being more interested in demons than in the Holy Spirit. Some assume we are unhealthy in our attitude, thinking everyone involved in this ministry goes around "witch-hunting" and "looking for demons" behind every tree or circumstance.

We admit freely that some in this ministry *do* blame demons for everything, instead of blaming themselves. Some, pretending to have "discerning of spirits," make a bad guess and say, "You have a spirit of ," and then proceed to "cast it out"—or claim to do so, anyway.

This kind of behavior may impress some but offend others. We must *know for certain* that demon activity is present before we start rebuking it and casting it out.

In every true move of the Spirit of God, enthusiastic people want to help without having the proper experience behind them. We must admit, however, that no one will ever learn anything unless he begins somewhere. Let's not be too hard on these enthusiasts. Novices should be involved under the direction of more experienced Christians.

Christians who are involved in the ministry of deliverance are not *looking* for demons. They are looking to bring healing and release to the thousands who are oppressed.

Exposing Themselves

When the Lord first opened my eyes to the reality of demons, I was *not* looking for them. My only motivation was to bring healing to a man who was chronically sick. Someone had advised me to change my method of praying. Instead of asking Jesus to heal the man, this person suggested that I might get better results by rebuking the sickness in Jesus' name.

The results were astonishing. I came face to face with demons *immediately.* But I was not *looking* for them. They reacted when challenged in the mighty name of Jesus. Many Christians, fearing the unknown, prefer to do nothing about demons. Our ignorance and inactivity allows them to remain hidden as they happily continue their evil work.

Demons always react when Jesus is preached in His fullness. Evil spirits often deceive people into believing they don't exist. Demons may hurl criticism or condemnation upon those who are casting them out.

During a worship service in Brooklyn, New York, a religious demon started to manifest itself by praising God in a falsetto voice. The face of the person was contorted in distress. I recognized the demon and cast it out at the end of the service. I was not looking for it. But the worship of God flushed it out of its hiding place and caused this demon to try to simulate praise.

What happened when Jesus went into the synagogue at Capernaum? Was He looking for demons? No, He was merely teaching doctrine when suddenly an unclean spirit cried out.

> But Jesus rebuked him, saying, "Be quiet, and
> come out of him!" And when the unclean spirit
> had convulsed him and cried out with a loud
> voice, he came out of him—Mark 1:25,26.

The evil spirit obeyed. The people in the synagogue were
undoubtedly astonished by those unusual events. Maybe if
Jesus had been more refined and diplomatic, He would have
avoided such an "unpleasant reaction" in the house of God!

No, we don't look for demons; but they are hiding until
we address them and cast them out—or until the presence
of the Lord stirs them up and they manifest themselves.

4. Can't demons be handled more effectively by simply praising God and ignoring them?

In the move of the Holy Spirit today, the necessity to praise
God is emphasized in many teachings. Biblical praise and
worship have been sadly lacking in the historic, denomina-
tional churches. But where true rejoicing is being practiced,
worshipers are discovering that "a merry heart does good,
like medicine" (Proverbs 17:22).

Are there any limits to our being thankful in this life?

> In everything give thanks; for this is the will of
> God in Christ Jesus for you—1 Thessalonians 5:18.

> Giving thanks always for all things to God the
> Father in the name of our Lord Jesus Christ—
> Ephesians 5:20.

Scripture tells us to give thanks *in* everything and *for*
everything. Demonstrating such an attitude in the face of
adversity will result in having a joyful spirit. By praising God,
we can certainly prevent evil spirits of despondency, jealousy, and criticism from robbing us of the victory of Calvary.

The doctrine of praise, however, does not replace the doctrine of deliverance. The two are distinctly separate, yet complimentary. In many cases, a person may be bound by a "spirit of heaviness" (Isaiah 61:3), and this must be replaced by the spirit of joy. Praising God from the heart is difficult if one is bound by a spirit of heaviness.

Heaviness and depression are characteristics of a demon spirit, while joy is a characteristic of the *Holy* Spirit. Heaviness must be cast out in the name of Jesus before the Holy Spirit can be prayed in. After the Holy Spirit comes in, the formerly afflicted person will find it much easier to worship God.

No Substitute

Let me add this warning. Praising God with a loud voice or with raised hands can be done in the energy of the flesh, and not from the inner recesses of the heart. This exercise will produce nothing except weariness. A display of fleshly effort will certainly not cast out spirits from one's person.

First, we must get to the point of thanking God *in* our suffering. Then we must resist any temptation to be sorry for ourselves and begin to praise God in the unpleasant situation; then we will encourage our spirits and minds to believe God for the ultimate deliverance.

Although I've ministered to charismatic groups who have been taught to praise, I've still had to cast out the binding spirits from them. Praise is no substitute for deliverance, although praise certainly makes it easier to resist Satan.

The first reaction after deliverance is almost always a strong desire to praise God. Sometimes, the person may be so overcome with emotion that their praising is seen in weeping—which is a little hard for unsaved people to understand!

Praise is good, but it's not a substitute for deliverance. If you are afflicted, start praising God and seek the help you need to be free from demonic oppression. We need to experience deliverance from bondage and freedom in worship if we are to be whole in body, mind, and spirit.

5. Doesn't the ministry of deliverance magnify the devil rather than Jesus Christ?

On the contrary, the ministry of deliverance demonstrates the defeat of the devil more plainly than any other ministry I know! When we cast out wicked spirits in the name and authority of Jesus, Jesus is magnified, certainly not Satan and his evil hordes.

When you "magnify" anything, you make it look bigger or greater. How does *casting out* demons make them look greater than Jesus Christ? If we can order demons to leave in the name of Jesus, and they obey, doesn't that demonstrate the *power* of Jesus and the *lack of power* of the devil?

Where do we get the idea that defeating demons and casting them out gives *any* glory to the devil? Strange kind of glory *that* is! Is it any glory to a man when he is fired from his job? Is it any glory to demons when they are expelled in the name of Jesus? Far from it, casting out demons shows what miserable, weak creatures they really are!

This question is usually asked by Christians who attend churches where the biblical command to "cast out devils" is not being obeyed. These believers have not been taught that Jesus defeated demons, sickness, and disease at Calvary. These uninformed Christians go through life believing that they are "bearing their cross" when oppression comes. How the devil must enjoy our appalling ignorance of the power of the gospel!

The Heart of the Gospel

What does Scripture say about Jesus' very purpose for coming to earth?

> For this purpose the Son of God was manifested, that He might destroy the works of the devil—1 John 3:8.

> God anointed Jesus of Nazareth with the Holy Spirit and with power, who went about doing good and healing all who were oppressed by the devil—Acts 10:38.

> Through death He [Jesus] might destroy him who had the power of death, that is, the devil, and release those who through fear of death were all their lifetime subject to bondage—Hebrews 2:14,15.

The very heart of the gospel is Jesus' power to deliver suffering humanity from the cruel oppression of the devil. This is to be done through the preaching of the Word, casting out demons, and healing the sick.

The gimmicks, contests, and "giveaways" used by many churches today to encourage Christian people to "win souls" is certainly not based on the Bible. Yet those who "play at the gospel" with such unscriptural means of reaching the lost scoff at those of us who take the command of Jesus seriously to "cast out devils"!

One of the early demonstrations of Jesus' power took place when He cast a demon out of a man at Capernaum. (See Mark 1:23-27.) Later, He gave His twelve disciples authority over all demons and power to cure all diseases. (See Luke 9:1.) Finally, He passed on this ministry of deliverance to the entire church, saying, "These signs will follow those who believe: In My name they will cast out demons . . ." (Mark 16:17).

The ministry of deliverance is not an unpleasant addition to the gospel. Casting out demons is one of the very *essential* ministries of those who preach the gospel. Praise God that the whole ministry of deliverance is being rediscovered in this present outpouring of the Holy Spirit! More and more Spirit-filled Christians are entering into the battle, and thousands are being set free.

6. Why blame the works of the flesh on demons?

Obviously, the temptations of the flesh are different from oppression by demons. If your problem is due to the weaknesses of the flesh, you can gain victory by dying to the desires of the flesh, trusting Jesus, and walking in the power of the Holy Spirit. But if your problem refuses to be conquered, then you may suspect the activity of demons.

These two kinds of problems are to be handled in two very different ways. The flesh is to be *crucified,* but demons are to be *cast out.* You cannot crucify a demon.

The Bible teaches us to bring the works of the flesh into subjection to Jesus Christ. We must "reckon" that our old Adamic nature, which is corrupt, is nailed to the cross of Jesus. This is a daily "reckoning."

> Reckon yourselves to be dead indeed to sin, but alive to God in Christ Jesus our Lord. Therefore do not let sin reign in your mortal body, that you should obey it in its lusts.
>
> And do not present your members as instruments of unrighteousness to sin, but present yourselves to God as being alive from the dead, and your members as instruments of righteousness to God—Romans 6:11-13.

Jesus can only live His life in a Christian's mortal body as He is given daily permission. But if that Christian gives his old fleshly nature back to Satan after reckoning it to be dead, then Satan will gladly take it again (or any portion of it). We must not blame the devil for our backslidings. We must blame ourselves.

Combatting the Works of the Flesh

The apostle Paul clearly warned the Galatians about the works of the flesh.

> Now the works of the flesh are evident, which are: adultery, fornication, uncleanness, licentiousness, idolatry, sorcery, hatred, contentions, jealousies, outbursts of wrath, selfish ambitions, dissensions, heresies, envy, murders, drunkenness, revelries, and the like; of which I tell you beforehand, just as I also told you in time past, that those who practice such things will not inherit the kingdom of God—Galatians 5:19-21.

The solution for combatting the works of the flesh is found in that same chapter. "I say then: Walk in the Spirit, and you shall not fulfill the lust of the flesh" (Galatians 5:16). Christians need to replace sinful behavior or habits with Spirit-led activity. Instead of stealing, a person needs to labor with his hands. Unwholesome speech needs to be replaced by words that edify. (See Ephesians 4:28,29.)

The apostle Paul also exhorted the early Christians to give "no place to the devil" (Ephesians 4:27, KJV). If we surrender any part of our old nature to the devil after conversion, he immediately takes what he can and plots to "install" a demon to continue the work of evil.

This is what happens when a Christian backslides. In cases where chronic backsliding has occurred, the tormented individual may need to call for the elders of the church to pray the prayer of faith and set him free from these demonic powers.

I am not saying that a Christian becomes oppressed by demons the moment he backslides and partakes of fleshly activity. But he is certainly making a way for Satan to occupy an area of his life. There is no other protection from demonic oppression except repenting immediately, pleading the blood of Jesus, and being restored to full fellowship with Jesus. Maintaining a close walk with God is essential to keeping your deliverance

7. If the ministry of deliverance is valid and scriptural, where has it been throughout the church age?

The writings of some of the early church fathers, such as Iranaeus, Polycarp, Justin Martyr, and Clement, indicate that each new convert normally experienced deliverance at conversion before being baptized in water. Ancient writings of the Roman Catholic Church reveal that certain priests had a ministry of deliverance, with coughings and manifestations similar to those we see in this ministry today.

Unfortunately, the church fell into apostasy with the passing of time. Despite losing its grip on many of the precious ministries and gifts of the Holy Spirit, the church began to recapture these truths through Martin Luther, the Wesley brothers, and other great evangelical leaders of the past century.

God continued to gradually restore forgotten truth. Justification by faith, baptism by immersion, and translating the Word of God into the language of the common people brought tremendous upheaval and change. At the turn of the twentieth century, the outpouring of the Holy Spirit revived speaking in tongues, prophesying, and the ministry of divine healing.

Halfway through this century, Christians began to realize that demons cause mental and physical sicknesses. Following the scriptural pattern of Christ and His disciples, we proceeded to cast demons out of afflicted individuals who sought relief from oppression. Deliverance meetings were met with scorn, especially by those groups that did not understand this ministry.

Cleaning Up the Church

Great opposition accompanied speaking in tongues at the turn of the century, but God still moved forward. Despite misunderstanding and opposition to the ministry of deliverance, God will still continue to move forward in victory.

Jesus Christ is preparing His church—His bride—to be without spot or wrinkle and to be prepared for His return. The bride needs a whole lot of "working over." Jesus is not returning for a Roman Catholic bride or a Protestant bride. He is returning for one Church, composed of blood-washed men and women who are filled with the Spirit. Like the parable of the five wise virgins, He is looking for those whose lamps are full of oil and burning brightly.

The day of denominations has ended. The only "world church" will be the *true* one that Jesus is now building in every nation. This is the day of cleansing—and that is why God is restoring the ministry of deliverance to the church.

Many Christians need deliverance from satanic oppression. We need not be fearful of exercising our rightful authority in Jesus Christ to set the captives free. Let us use it to prepare the body of Christ for the last phase of the church age.

8. Wouldn't it be better to cast the demons out of ourselves, rather than worrying about the demons in others?

Some of the people who ask this question feel that "demon" is a dirty word, and that deliverance is such an embarrassing and private matter that they would far rather "deliver themselves" than ask for the prayers of someone else!

On the other hand, some people are concerned about the whole question of deliverance from another standpoint: they ask themselves, "How will it affect my attitude toward my Christian friend if I begin to believe that he is oppressed by a demon? Won't that block fellowship? Won't that make me unnecessarily wary of him? Wouldn't it be better for me not to entertain such thoughts, and just keep my own backyard clean?''

Let's address the second question first. If a friend of yours is obviously being oppressed by a demon, you do him no favor by ignoring his problem and acting like it doesn't exist!

If you truly love him as a brother in Christ, then you ought to spend time with him in prayer and fellowship until he comes to an understanding of his problem. When he is ready for deliverance, you ought to be the first to extend the helping hand, either by casting out the demon yourself or by taking him to a man or woman of God who practices this kind of ministry.

Another Christian should never be excluded from your fellowship just because he is being oppressed by a demon. Despite being under attack by Satan, he is a brother who also has the Holy Spirit in him. If there ever is a time when a person needs fellowship, it's when he's being oppressed by the devil. Don't sin against your Christian brother by ignoring his problems. Reach out in love and set the captive free in the name of Jesus.

Delivering Yourself?

Let me answer the first question about "delivering yourself." I agree that Christians can deliver themselves of demonic oppression—and many have done so. For some people, however, it *may* be a disturbing experience.

We know one lawyer in Michigan who heard teaching on deliverance and decided to try it on himself while driving home. As soon as he verbally rebuked the spirits in himself and commanded them to come out in Jesus' name, he immediately became nauseated. Not expecting that, he zipped into his driveway just in time, tumbled out of the car, and vomited on his front lawn! Later on, when he shared

his experience with us, I reminded him that having someone else minister to him might have been much easier!

If submitting yourself to the ministry of deliverance seems
somewhat embarrassing, just remember that this may be
exactly the kind of humility that some of us need in order
to be set free. Perhaps this is the reason the apostle James
tells us to "Confess your trespasses to one another, and pray
for one another, that you may be healed" (James 5:16).

Notice that confession of sin, which is a difficult if not
embarrassing thing to do, precedes praying for one another.
Once we have confessed our needs and our faults to one
another, it is much easier to pray the prayer of faith. Remember, the prayer of *faith,* not the prayer of uncertainty, brings
results.

9. If the great archangel Michael dared not re-
buke Satan, who are we that we may do so?

This question is frequently asked by those who do not
understand our amazing authority in Christ. Let's look at
the passage upon which this argument is based.

> Yet Michael the archangel, in contending with the
> devil, when he disputed about the body of Moses,
> dared not bring against him a reviling accusation,
> but said, "The Lord rebuke you!"—Jude 9.

If this great archangel, who is the helper of all Christians
(see Daniel 12:1), dared not bring any criticism or accusa-
tion against Satan, how is it that *we* can openly and pugna-
ciously rebuke the devil?

In the beginning, God made man after His own image—
but *a little lower* than the angels. (See Psalm 8:5.) When
Jesus, made in the likeness of sinful man, took man's place
on the cross and died for the whole world, He defeated Satan
completely and totally for all time.

Any person who trusts in Christ automatically becomes a son of God, raised to a much higher level than was possible in Old Testament days. In Old Testament times, the angels were higher than men; but *after* the cross, believers were elevated higher than angels, including Satan himself.

The Authority of the Believer

God the Father raised Jesus from the cross to the position of supreme conqueror, and put Him at His right hand on His throne. Christ is seated in heavenly places "far above all principality and power and might and dominion, and every name that is named, not only in this age but also in that which is to come" (Ephesians 1:21). All the defeated enemies are now under Jesus' feet.

Positionally, we are *in Christ,* and therefore we share in His victory. According to the words of Jesus, we may also put *our* feet on these angelic and demon powers.

> Behold, I give unto you power [*exousia:* authority] to tread on serpents and scorpions, and over all the power [*dunamis:* ability] of the enemy: and nothing shall by any means hurt you—Luke 10:19, KJV.

Jesus was raised to sit in heavenly places by His Father, and is authorized to elevate us also, as we abide in Him. We may exercise His power and authority without any fear of reprisals from our adversary, the devil.

Most people are unaware of this authority vested in Christians and, therefore, do not use it. Others are aware of it, but may be afraid to exercise it lest they get a "kick back." Their fear and inactivity allows Satan to continue his dirty work unopposed.

Too often we pray but do not take our authority. Jesus did not tell us to pray for *Him* to rebuke the devil. He did that on the cross. He tells *us* to rebuke the enemy in His name. We become an extension of Jesus on earth as members of His Body—flesh of His flesh and bone of His bone. (See Ephesians 5:30.)

Jesus did not die for angels. He died for humans. Angels have become our servants to help us exercise the ministry of Jesus here on earth. (See Hebrews 1:14.) If He cast out demons (fallen angels), we may do the same.

We now possess His power of attorney, and we must do as He commanded us:

> "And as you go, preach, saying, 'The kingdom of God is at hand.' Heal the sick, cleanse the lepers, raise the dead, cast out demons. Freely you have received, freely give"—Matthew 10:7,8.

The work of every minister of the New Testament gospel is summed up in this commission. If we preach without healing and casting out demons in His name, we are simply saying, to our everlasting shame, that we know a better way to preach the gospel.

For more information write to:

Pastor Stephen Whyte
2 Delbert Drive
Scarborough, Ontario
Canada M1P 1X1